Summary

Introduced in House (07/24/2017)

Countering America's Adversaries Through Sanctions Act

Countering Iran's Destabilizing Activities Act of 2017

This bill directs the President to impose sanctions against: (1) Iran's ballistic missile or weapons of mass destruction programs, (2) the sale or transfer to Iran of military equipment or the provision of related technical or financial assistance, and (3) Iran's Islamic Revolutionary Guard Corps and affiliated foreign persons.

The President may impose sanctions against persons responsible for violations of internationally recognized human rights committed against individuals in Iran.

The President may temporarily waive the imposition or continuation of sanctions under specified circumstances.

Countering Russian Influence in Europe and Eurasia Act of 2017

The President must submit for congressional review certain proposed actions to terminate or waive sanctions with respect to the Russian Federation.

Specified executive order sanctions against Russia shall remain in effect.

The President may waive specified cyber- and Ukraine-related sanctions.

The bill provides sanctions for activities concerning: (1) cyber security, (2) crude oil projects, (3) financial institutions, (4) corruption, (5) human rights abuses, (6) evasion of sanctions, (7) transactions with Russian defense or intelligence sectors, (8) export pipelines, (9) privatization of state-owned assets by government officials, and (10) arms transfers to Syria.

The Department of State shall work with the government of Ukraine to increase Ukraine's energy security.

The bill: (1) directs the Department of the Treasury to develop a national strategy for combating the financing of terrorism, and (2) includes the Secretary of the Treasury on the National Security Council.

Korean Interdiction and Modernization of Sanctions Act

The bill modifies and increases the President's authority to impose sanctions on persons in violation of certain United Nations Security Council resolutions regarding North Korea.

U.S. financial institutions shall not establish or maintain correspondent accounts used by foreign financial institutions to provide indirect financial services to North Korea.

A foreign government that provides to or receives from North Korea a defense article or service is prohibited from receiving certain types of U.S. foreign assistance.

The bill provides sanctions against: (1) North Korean cargo and shipping, (2) goods produced in whole or part by North Korean convict or forced labor, and (3) foreign persons that employ North Korean forced laborers.

The State Department shall submit a determination regarding whether North Korea meets the criteria for designation as a state sponsor of terrorism.

Sponsor: Rep. Royce, Edward R. [R-CA-39]

Cosponsors:

Rep. Engel, Eliot L. [D-NY-16]*

Rep. McCarthy, Kevin [R-CA-23]*

Rep. Hoyer, Steny H. [D-MD-5]*

Rep. Cohen, Steve [D-TN-9]

Rep. Smith, Christopher H. [R-NJ-4]

Edited BY
Okonkwo Gerald

H.R.3364 - Countering America's Adversaries Through Sanctions Act115th Congress (2017-2018)

Law

Sponsor: Rep. Royce, Edward R. [R-CA-39]
(Introduced 07/24/2017)

Committees: House - Foreign Affairs; Intelligence (Permanent); Judiciary; Oversight and Government Reform; Armed Services; Financial Services; Rules; Ways and Means; Transportation and Infrastructure

Latest Action: 08/02/2017 Became Public Law No: 115-44

Roll Call Votes: There have been 2 roll call votes

This bill has the status Became Law

HERE ARE THE STEPS FOR STATUS OF LEGISLATION:

1. *Introduced*
2. *Passed House*
3. *Passed Senate*
4. *To President*
5. *Became Law*

One Hundred Fifteenth Congress
of the
United States of America

AT THE FIRST SESSION

Begun and held at the City of Washington on Tuesday,
the third day of January, two thousand and seventeen

An Act

To provide congressional review and to counter
aggression by the Governments of Iran, the
Russian Federation, and North Korea, and for
other purposes.

Be it enacted by the Senate and House of
Representatives of the United States of America in
Congress assembled,

SECTION 1. SHORT TITLE; TABLE OF CONTENTS.

(a) SHORT TITLE.—This Act may be cited as the
"Countering America's Adversaries Through Sanctions
Act".

(b) TABLE OF CONTENTS.—The table of contents
for this Act is as follows:

TITLE I—SANCTIONS WITH RESPECT TO IRAN

TITLE II—SANCTIONS WITH RESPECT TO THE RUSSIAN FEDERATION AND COMBATING TERRORISM AND ILLICIT FINANCING

PART 3—REPORTS

Subtitle B—Countering Russian influence in

Europe and Eurasia

Subtitle C—Combating terrorism and illicit financing

PART 1—NATIONAL STRATEGY FOR COMBATING TERRORIST AND OTHER ILLICIT FINANCING

PART 2—ENHANCING ANTITERRORISM TOOLS OF THE DEPARTMENT OF THE TREASURY

PART 3—DEFINITIONS

Subtitle D—Rule of construction

TITLE III—SANCTIONS WITH RESPECT TO NORTH KOREA

Subtitle A—Sanctions to enforce and implement United Nations Security Council sanctions against North Korea

TITLE I—SANCTIONS WITH RESPECT TO IRAN

SEC. 101. SHORT TITLE.

This title may be cited as the "Countering Iran's Destabilizing Activities Act of 2017".

SEC. 102. DEFINITIONS.

In this title:

(1) **ACT OF INTERNATIONAL TERRORISM.—** The term "act of international terrorism" has the meaning given that term in section 14 of the Iran Sanctions Act of 1996 (Public Law 104–172; 50 U.S.C. 1701 note).

(2) **APPROPRIATE CONGRESSIONAL COMMITTEES.—**The term "appropriate congressional committees" has the meaning given that term in section 14 of the Iran Sanctions Act of 1996 (Public Law 104–172; 50 U.S.C. 1701 note).

(3) **FOREIGN PERSON.—**The term "foreign person" means a person that is not a United States person.

(4) **IRANIAN PERSON.—**The term "Iranian person" means—

(A) an individual who is a citizen or national of Iran; or

(B) an entity organized under the laws of Iran or otherwise subject to the jurisdiction of the Government of Iran.

(5) **IRGC.**—The term **"IRGC"** means Iran's Islamic Revolutionary Guard Corps.

(6) **KNOWINGLY**.—The term "knowingly" has the meaning given that term in section 14 of the Iran Sanctions Act of 1996 (Public Law 104–172; 50 U.S.C. 1701 note).

(7) **UNITED STATES PERSON**.—The term "United States person" means—

(A) a United States citizen or an alien lawfully admitted for permanent residence to the United States; or

(B) an entity organized under the laws of the United States or of any jurisdiction within the United States, including a foreign branch of such an entity.

SEC. 103. REGIONAL STRATEGY FOR COUNTERING CONVENTIONAL AND ASYMMETRIC IRANIAN THREATS IN THE MIDDLE EAST AND NORTH AFRICA.

(a) IN GENERAL.—Not later than 180 days after the date of the enactment of this Act, and every 2 years thereafter, the Secretary of State, the Secretary of Defense, the Secretary of the Treasury, and the Director of National Intelligence shall jointly develop and submit to the appropriate congressional committees and leadership a strategy for deterring conventional and asymmetric Iranian activities and threats that directly threaten the United States and key allies in the Middle East, North Africa, and beyond.

(b) ELEMENTS.—The strategy required by subsection (a) shall include at a minimum the following:

(1) A summary of the near- and long-term United States objectives, plans, and means for countering Iran's destabilizing activities, including identification of countries that share the objective of countering Iran's destabilizing activities.

(2) A summary of the capabilities and contributions of individual countries to shared efforts to counter Iran's destabilizing activities, and a summary of additional actions or contributions that each country could take to further contribute.

(3) An assessment of Iran's conventional force capabilities and an assessment of Iran's plans to upgrade its conventional force capabilities, including its acquisition, development, and deployment of ballistic and cruise missile capabilities, unmanned aerial vehicles, and maritime offensive and anti-access or area denial capabilities.

(4) An assessment of Iran's chemical and biological weapons capabilities and an assessment of Iranian plans to upgrade its chemical or biological weapons capabilities.

(5) An assessment of Iran's asymmetric activities in the region, including—

(A) the size, capabilities, and activities of the IRGC, including the Quds Force;

(B) the size, capabilities, and activities of Iran's cyber operations;

(C) the types and amount of support, including funding, lethal and nonlethal contributions, and training, provided to Hezbollah, Hamas, special groups in Iraq, the regime of Bashar al-Assad in Syria, Houthi fighters in Yemen, and other violent groups across the Middle East; and

(D) The scope and objectives of Iran's information operations and use of propaganda.

(6) A summary of United States actions, unilaterally and in cooperation with foreign governments, to counter destabilizing Iranian activities, including—

(A) interdiction of Iranian lethal arms bound for groups designated as foreign terrorist organizations under section 219 of the Immigration and Nationality Act (8 U.S.C. 1189);

(B) Iran's interference in international commercial shipping lanes;

(C) attempts by Iran to undermine or subvert internationally recognized governments in the Middle East region; and

(D) Iran's support for the regime of Bashar al-Assad in Syria, including—

(i) financial assistance, military equipment and

personnel, and other support provided to that regime; and

(ii) support and direction to other armed actors that are not Syrian or Iranian and are acting on behalf of that regime.

(c) FORM OF STRATEGY.—The strategy required by subsection (a) shall be submitted in unclassified form, but may include a classified annex.

(d) APPROPRIATE CONGRESSIONAL COMMITTEES AND LEADERSHIP DEFINED.—In this section, the term "appropriate congressional committees and leadership" means—

(1) the Committee on Finance, the Committee on Banking, Housing, and Urban Affairs, the Committee on Foreign Relations, and the majority and minority leaders of the Senate; and

(2) the Committee on Ways and Means, the Committee on Financial Services, the Committee on Foreign Affairs, and the Speaker, the majority leader, and the minority leader of the House of Representatives.

SEC. 104. IMPOSITION OF ADDITIONAL SANCTIONS IN RESPONSE TO IRAN'S BALLISTIC MISSILE PROGRAM.

(a) SENSE OF CONGRESS.—It is the sense of Congress that the Secretary of the Treasury and the Secretary of State should continue to implement

Executive Order No. 13382 (50 U.S.C. 1701 note; relating to blocking property of weapons of mass destruction delivery system proliferators and their supporters).

(b) IMPOSITION OF SANCTIONS.—The President shall impose the sanctions described in subsection (c) with respect to any person that the President determines, on or after the date of the enactment of this Act—

(1) knowingly engages in any activity that materially contributes to the activities of the Government of Iran with respect to its ballistic missile program, or any other program in Iran for developing, deploying, or maintaining systems capable of delivering weapons of mass destruction, including any efforts to manufacture, acquire, possess, develop, transport, transfer, or use such capabilities;

(2) is a successor entity to a person referred to in paragraph (1);

(3) owns or controls or is owned or controlled by a person referred to in paragraph (1);

(4) forms an entity with the purpose of evading sanctions that would otherwise be imposed pursuant to paragraph (3);

(5) is acting for or on behalf of a person referred to in paragraph (1), (2), (3), or (4); or

(6) knowingly provides or attempts to provide financial, material, technological, or other support for, or goods or services in support of, a person referred to

in paragraph (1), (2), (3), (4) or (5).

(c) SANCTIONS DESCRIBED.—The sanctions described in this subsection are the following:

(1) BLOCKING OF PROPERTY.—The President shall block, in accordance with the International Emergency Economic Powers Act (50 U.S.C. 1701 et seq.), all transactions in all property and interests in property of any person subject to subsection (b) if such property and interests in property are in the United States, come within the United States, or are or come within the possession or control of a United States person.

(2) EXCLUSION FROM UNITED STATES.—The Secretary of State shall deny a visa to, and the Secretary of Homeland Security shall exclude from the United States, any person subject to subsection (b) that is an alien.

(d) PENALTIES.—A person that violates, attempts to violate, conspires to violate, or causes a violation of subsection (c)(1) or any regulation, license, or order issued to carry out that subsection shall be subject to the penalties set forth in subsections (b) and (c) of section 206 of the International Emergency Economic Powers Act (50 U.S.C. 1705) to the same extent as a person that commits an unlawful act described in subsection (a) of that section.

(e) **REPORT ON CONTRIBUTIONS TO IRAN'S BALLISTIC MISSILE PROGRAM.—**

(1) IN GENERAL.—Not later than 180 days after the date of the enactment of this Act, and every 180 days thereafter, the President shall submit to the appropriate congressional committees a report describing each person that—

(A) has, during the period specified in paragraph (2), conducted any activity that has materially contributed to the activities of the Government of Iran with respect to its ballistic missile program, or any other program in Iran for developing, deploying, or maintaining systems capable of delivering weapons of mass destruction, including any efforts to manufacture, acquire, possess, develop, transport, transfer, or use such capabilities;

(B) is a successor entity to a person referred to in subparagraph (A);

(C) owns or controls or is owned or controlled by a person referred to in subparagraph (A);

(D) forms an entity with the purpose of evading sanctions that could be imposed as a result of a relationship described in subparagraph (C);

(E) is acting for or on behalf of a person referred to in subparagraph (A), (B), (C), or (D); or

(F) is known or believed to have provided, or attempted to provide, during the period specified in paragraph (2), financial, material, technological, or other support for, or goods or services in support of, any material contribution to a program described in subparagraph (A) carried out by a person described in subparagraph (A), (B), (C), (D), or (E).

(2) PERIOD SPECIFIED.—The period specified in this paragraph is—

(A) in the case of the first report submitted under paragraph (1), the period beginning January 1, 2016, and ending on the date the report is submitted; and

(B) in the case of a subsequent such report, the 180-day period preceding the submission of the report.

(3) FORM OF REPORT.—Each report required by paragraph (1) shall be submitted in unclassified form but may include a classified annex.

SEC. 105. IMPOSITION OF TERRORISM-RELATED SANCTIONS WITH RESPECT TO THE IRGC.

(a) FINDINGS.—Congress makes the following findings:

(1) The **IRGC** is subject to sanctions pursuant to Executive Order No. 13382 (50 U.S.C. 1701 note; relating to blocking property of weapons of mass destruction delivery system proliferators and their supporters), the Comprehensive Iran Sanctions, Accountability, and Divestment Act of 2010 (22 U.S.C. 8501 et seq.), Executive Order No. 13553 (50 U.S.C. 1701 note; relating to blocking property of certain persons with respect to serious human rights abuses by the Government of Iran), and Executive Order No. 13606 (50 U.S.C. 1701 note; relating to blocking the property and suspending entry into the United States of certain persons with respect to grave human rights abuses by the Governments of Iran and Syria via information technology).

(2) The Iranian Revolutionary Guard Corps–Quds Force (in this section referred to as the "IRGC–QF") is the primary arm of the Government of Iran for executing its policy of supporting terrorist and insurgent groups. The IRGC–QF provides material, logistical assistance, training, and financial support to militants and terrorist operatives throughout the Middle East and South Asia and was designated for the imposition of sanctions by the Secretary of the Treasury pursuant to Executive Order No. 13224 (50 U.S.C. 1701 note; relating to blocking property and prohibiting transactions with persons who commit, threaten to commit, or support terrorism) in October 2007 for its support of terrorism.

(3) The IRGC, not just the IRGC–QF, is responsible for implementing Iran's international program of destabilizing activities, support for acts of international terrorism, and ballistic missile program.

(b) IN GENERAL.—Beginning on the date that is 90 days after the date of the enactment of this Act, the President shall impose the sanctions described in subsection (c) with respect to the IRGC and foreign persons that are officials, agents, or affiliates of the IRGC.

(c) SANCTIONS DESCRIBED.—The sanctions described in this subsection are sanctions applicable with respect to a foreign person pursuant to Executive Order No. 13224 (50 U.S.C. 1701 note; relating to blocking property and prohibiting transactions with persons who commit, threaten to commit, or support terrorism).

SEC. 106. IMPOSITION OF ADDITIONAL SANCTIONS WITH RESPECT TO PERSONS RESPONSIBLE FOR HUMAN RIGHTS ABUSES.

(a) **IN GENERAL.**—Not later than 90 days after the date of the enactment of this Act, and annually thereafter, the Secretary of State shall submit to the appropriate congressional committees a list of each person the Secretary determines, based on credible evidence, on or after the date of the enactment of this Act—

(1) is responsible for extrajudicial killings, torture, or other gross violations of internationally recognized human rights committed against individuals in Iran who seek—

(A) to expose illegal activity carried out by officials of the Government of Iran; or

(B) to obtain, exercise, defend, or promote internationally recognized human rights and freedoms, such as the freedoms of religion, expression, association, and assembly, and the rights to a fair trial and democratic elections; or

(2) acts as an agent of or on behalf of a foreign person in a matter relating to an activity described in paragraph (1).

(b) **SANCTIONS DESCRIBED.**—

(1) IN GENERAL.—The President may, in accordance with the International Emergency Economic Powers Act (50 U.S.C. 1701 et seq.), block all transactions in

all property and interests in property of a person on the list required by subsection (a) if such property and interests in property are in the United States, come within the United States, or are or come within the possession or control of a United States person.

(2) PENALTIES.—A person that violates, attempts to violate, conspires to violate, or causes a violation of paragraph (1) or any regulation, license, or order issued to carry out paragraph (1) shall be subject to the penalties set forth in subsections (b) and (c) of section 206 of the International Emergency Economic Powers Act (50 U.S.C. 1705) to the same extent as a person that commits an unlawful act described in subsection (a) of that section.

SEC. 107. ENFORCEMENT OF ARMS EMBARGOS.

(a) **IN GENERAL.**—Except as provided in subsection (d), the President shall impose the sanctions described in subsection (b) with respect to any person that the President determines—

(1) knowingly engages in any activity that materially contributes to the supply, sale, or transfer directly or indirectly to or from Iran, or for the use in or benefit of Iran, of any battle tanks, armored combat vehicles, large caliber artillery systems, combat aircraft, attack helicopters, warships, missiles or missile systems, as defined for the purpose of the United Nations Register of Conventional Arms, or related materiel, including spare parts; or

(2) knowingly provides to Iran any technical training, financial resources or services, advice, other services or assistance related to the supply, sale, transfer, manufacture, maintenance, or use of arms and related materiel described in paragraph (1).

(b) SANCTIONS DESCRIBED.—

(1) **BLOCKING OF PROPERTY.**—The President shall block, in accordance with the International Emergency Economic Powers Act (50 U.S.C. 1701 et seq.), all transactions in all property and interests in property of any person subject to subsection (a) if such property and interests in property are in the United States, come within the United States, or are or come within the possession or control of a United States person.

(2) **EXCLUSION FROM UNITED STATES.**—The Secretary of State shall deny a visa to, and the Secretary of Homeland Security shall exclude from the United States, any person subject to subsection (a) that is an alien.

(c) PENALTIES.—A person that violates, attempts to violate, conspires to violate, or causes a violation of subsection (b)(1) or any regulation, license, or order issued to carry out that subsection shall be subject to the penalties set forth in subsections (b) and (c) of section 206 of the International Emergency Economic Powers Act (50 U.S.C. 1705) to the same extent as a person that commits an unlawful act described in subsection (a) of that section.

(d) EXCEPTION.—The President is not required to impose sanctions under subsection (a) with respect to a person for engaging in an activity described in that subsection if the President certifies to the appropriate congressional committees that—

(1) permitting the activity is in the national security interest of the United States;

(2) Iran no longer presents a significant threat to the national security of the United States and to the allies of the United States; and

(3) the Government of Iran has ceased providing operational or financial support for acts of international terrorism and no longer satisfies the requirements for designation as a state sponsor of terrorism.

(e) STATE SPONSOR OF TERRORISM DEFINED.—In this section, the term "state sponsor of terrorism" means a country the government of which the Secretary of State has determined to be a government that has repeatedly provided support for acts of international terrorism for purposes of—

(1) section 6(j)(1)(A) of the Export Administration Act of 1979 (50 U.S.C. 4605(j)(1)(A)) (as continued in effect pursuant to the International Emergency Economic Powers Act (50 U.S.C. 1701 et seq.));

(2) section 620A(a) of the Foreign Assistance Act of 1961 (22 U.S.C. 2371(a));

(3) section 40(d) of the Arms Export Control Act (22 U.S.C. 2780(d)); or

(4) any other provision of law.

SEC. 108. REVIEW OF APPLICABILITY OF SANCTIONS RELATING TO IRAN'S SUPPORT FOR TERRORISM AND ITS BALLISTIC MISSILE PROGRAM.

(a) IN GENERAL.—Not later than 5 years after the date of the enactment of this Act, the President shall conduct a review of all persons on the list of specially designated nationals and blocked persons maintained by the Office of Foreign Assets Control of the Department of the Treasury for activities relating to Iran—

(1) to assess the conduct of such persons as that conduct relates to—

(A) any activity that materially contributes to the activities of the Government of Iran with respect to its ballistic missile program; or

(B) support by the Government of Iran for acts of international terrorism; and

(2) to determine the applicability of sanctions with respect to such persons under—

(A) Executive Order No. 13382 (50 U.S.C. 1701 note; relating to blocking property of weapons of mass destruction delivery system proliferators and their supporters); or

(B) Executive Order No. 13224 (50 U.S.C. 1701 note; relating to blocking property and prohibiting transactions with persons who commit, threaten to commit, or support terrorism).

(b) IMPLEMENTATION OF SANCTIONS.—If the President determines under subsection (a) that sanctions under an Executive order specified in paragraph (2) of that subsection are applicable with respect to a person, the President shall—

(1) impose sanctions with respect to that person pursuant to that Executive order; or

(2) exercise the waiver authority provided under section 112.

SEC. 109. REPORT ON COORDINATION OF SANCTIONS BETWEEN THE UNITED STATES AND THE EUROPEAN UNION.

(a) IN GENERAL.—Not later than 180 days after the date of the enactment of this Act, and every 180 days thereafter, the President shall submit to the appropriate congressional committees a report that includes the following:

(1) A description of each instance, during the period specified in subsection (b)—

(A) in which the United States has imposed sanctions with respect to a person for activity related to the proliferation of weapons of mass destruction or delivery systems for such weapons to or by Iran, support for acts of international terrorism by Iran, or human rights abuses in Iran, but in which the European Union has not imposed corresponding sanctions; and

(B) in which the European Union has imposed sanctions with respect to a person for activity related to the proliferation of weapons of mass destruction or delivery systems for such weapons to or by Iran, support for acts of international terrorism by Iran, or human rights abuses in Iran, but in which the United States has not imposed corresponding sanctions.

(2) An explanation for the reason for each discrepancy between sanctions imposed by the European Union and sanctions imposed by the United States described in subparagraphs (A) and (B) of paragraph (1).

(b) PERIOD SPECIFIED.—The period specified in this subsection is—

(1) in the case of the first report submitted under subsection (a), the period beginning on the date of the enactment of this Act and ending on the date the report is submitted; and

(2) in the case of a subsequent such report, the 180-day period preceding the submission of the report.

(c) FORM OF REPORT.—The report required by subsection (a) shall be submitted in unclassified form but may include a classified annex.

SEC. 110. REPORT ON UNITED STATES CITIZENS DETAINED BY IRAN.

(a) IN GENERAL.—Not later than 90 days after the date of the enactment of this Act, and every 180 days thereafter, the President shall submit to the appropriate congressional committees and leadership a report on United States citizens, including United States citizens who are also citizens of other countries, detained by Iran or groups supported by Iran that includes—

(1) information regarding any officials of the Government of Iran involved in any way in the detentions; and

(2) a summary of efforts the United States Government has taken to secure the swift release of those United States citizens.

(b) FORM OF REPORT.—The report required by subsection (a) shall be submitted in unclassified form, but may include a classified annex.

(c) APPROPRIATE CONGRESSIONAL COMMITTEES AND LEADERSHIP DEFINED.—In this section, the term "appropriate congressional committees and leadership" means—

(1) the Committee on Finance, the Committee on Banking, Housing, and Urban Affairs, the Committee on Foreign Relations, and the majority and minority leaders of the Senate; and

(2) the Committee on Ways and Means, the Committee on Financial Services, the Committee on Foreign Affairs, and the Speaker, the majority leader, and the minority leader of the House of Representatives.

SEC. 111. EXCEPTIONS FOR NATIONAL SECURITY AND HUMANITARIAN

ASSISTANCE; RULE OF CONSTRUCTION.

(a) IN GENERAL.—The following activities shall be exempt from sanctions under sections 104, 105, 106, and 107:

(1) Any activity subject to the reporting requirements under title V of the National Security Act of 1947 (50 U.S.C. 3091 et seq.), or to any authorized intelligence activities of the United States.

(2) The admission of an alien to the United States if such admission is necessary to comply with United States obligations under the Agreement between the United Nations and the United States of America regarding the Headquarters of the United Nations, signed at Lake Success June 26, 1947, and entered into force November 21, 1947, or under the Convention on Consular Relations, done at Vienna April 24, 1963, and entered into force March 19, 1967, or other applicable international obligations of the United States.

(3) The conduct or facilitation of a transaction for the sale of agricultural commodities, food, medicine, or medical devices to Iran or for the provision of humanitarian assistance to the people of Iran, including engaging in a financial transaction relating to humanitarian assistance or for humanitarian purposes or transporting goods or services that are necessary to carry out operations relating to humanitarian assistance or humanitarian purposes.

(b) IMPLEMENTATION.—The President may exercise all authorities provided under sections 203 and 205 of the International Emergency Economic Powers Act (50 U.S.C. 1702 and 1704) to carry out this Act.

(c) RULE OF CONSTRUCTION.—Nothing in this Act shall be construed to limit the authority of the President under the International Emergency Economic Powers Act (50 U.S.C. 1701 et seq.).

(d) DEFINITIONS.—In this section:

(1) AGRICULTURAL COMMODITY.—The term "agricultural commodity" has the meaning given that term in section 102 of the Agricultural Trade Act of 1978 (7 U.S.C. 5602).

(2) GOOD.—The term "good" has the meaning given that term in section 16 of the Export Administration Act of 1979 (50 U.S.C. 4618) (as continued in effect pursuant to the International Emergency Economic Powers Act (50 U.S.C. 1701 et seq.)).

(3) MEDICAL DEVICE.—The term "medical device" has the meaning given the term "device" in section 201 of the Federal Food, Drug, and Cosmetic Act (21 U.S.C. 321).

(4) MEDICINE.—The term "medicine" has the meaning given the term "drug" in section 201 of the Federal Food, Drug, and Cosmetic Act (21 U.S.C. 321).

SEC. 112. PRESIDENTIAL WAIVER AUTHORITY.

(a) CASE-BY-CASE WAIVER AUTHORITY.—

(1) IN GENERAL.—The President may waive, on a case-by-case basis and for a period of not more than 180 days, a requirement under section 104, 105, 106, 107, or 108 to impose or maintain sanctions with respect to a person, and may waive the continued imposition of such sanctions, not less than 30 days after the President determines and reports to the appropriate congressional committees that it is vital to the national security interests of the United States to waive such sanctions.

(2) RENEWAL OF WAIVERS.—The President may, on a case-by-case basis, renew a waiver under paragraph (1) for an additional period of not more than 180 days if, not later than 15 days before that waiver expires, the President makes the determination and submits to the appropriate congressional committees a report described in paragraph (1).

(3) SUCCESSIVE RENEWAL.—The renewal authority provided under paragraph (2) may be exercised for additional successive periods of not more than 180 days if the President follows the procedures set forth in paragraph (2), and submits the report described in paragraph (1), for each such renewal.

(b) CONTENTS OF WAIVER REPORTS.—Each report submitted under subsection (a) in connection with a waiver of sanctions under section 104, 105, 106, 107, or 108 with respect to a person, or the renewal of such a waiver, shall include—

(1) a specific and detailed rationale for the determination that the waiver is vital to the national security interests of the United States;

(2) a description of the activity that resulted in the person being subject to sanctions;

(3) an explanation of any efforts made by the United States, as applicable, to secure the cooperation of the government with primary jurisdiction over the person or the location where the activity described in paragraph (2) occurred in terminating or, as appropriate, penalizing the activity; and

(4) an assessment of the significance of the activity described in paragraph (2) in contributing to the ability of Iran to threaten the interests of the United States or allies of the United States, develop systems capable of delivering weapons of mass destruction, support acts of international terrorism, or violate the human rights of any person in Iran.

(c) EFFECT OF REPORT ON WAIVER.—If the President submits a report under subsection (a) in connection with a waiver of sanctions under section 104, 105, 106, 107, or 108 with respect to a person, or the renewal of such a waiver, the President shall not be required to impose or maintain sanctions under section 104, 105, 106, 107, or 108, as applicable, with respect to the person described in the report during the 30-day period referred to in subsection (a).

TITLE II—SANCTIONS WITH RESPECT TO THE RUSSIAN FEDERATION AND

COMBATING TERRORISM AND ILLICIT FINANCING

SEC. 201. SHORT TITLE.

This title may be cited as the "Countering Russian Influence in Europe and Eurasia Act of 2017".

subtitle A—Sanctions and other measures with respect to the Russian Federation

SEC. 211. FINDINGS.

Congress makes the following findings:

(1) On March 6, 2014, President Barack Obama issued Executive Order No. 13660 (79 Fed. Reg. 13493; relating to blocking property of certain persons contributing to the situation in Ukraine), which authorizes the Secretary of the Treasury, in consultation with the Secretary of State, to impose sanctions on those determined to be undermining democratic processes and institutions in Ukraine or threatening the peace, security, stability, sovereignty, and territorial integrity of Ukraine. President Obama subsequently issued Executive Order No. 13661 (79 Fed. Reg. 15535; relating to blocking property of additional persons contributing to the situation in Ukraine) and Executive Order No. 13662 (79 Fed. Reg. 16169; relating to blocking property of additional persons contributing to the situation in Ukraine) to expand sanctions on certain persons contributing to the situation in Ukraine.

(2) On December 18, 2014, the Ukraine Freedom Support Act of 2014 was enacted (Public Law 113–272; 22 U.S.C. 8921 et seq.), which includes provisions directing the President to impose sanctions on foreign persons that the President determines to be entities owned or controlled by the Government of the Russian Federation or nationals of the Russian Federation that manufacture, sell, transfer, or otherwise provide certain defense articles into Syria.

(3) On April 1, 2015, President Obama issued Executive Order No. 13694 (80 Fed. Reg. 18077; relating to blocking the property of certain persons engaging in significant malicious cyber-enabled activities), which authorizes the Secretary of the Treasury, in consultation with the Attorney General and the Secretary of State, to impose sanctions on persons determined to be engaged in malicious cyber-hacking.

(4) On July 26, 2016, President Obama approved a Presidential Policy Directive on United States Cyber Incident Coordination, which states, "certain cyber incidents that have significant impacts on an entity, our national security, or the broader economy require a unique approach to response efforts".

(5) On December 29, 2016, President Obama issued an annex to Executive Order No. 13694, which authorized sanctions on the following entities and individuals:

(A) The Main Intelligence Directorate (also known as Glavnoe Razvedyvatel'noe Upravlenie or the GRU) in Moscow, Russian Federation.

(B) The Federal Security Service (also known as

Federalnaya Sluzhba Bezopasnosti or the FSB) in Moscow, Russian Federation.

(C) The Special Technology Center (also known as STLC, Ltd. Special Technology Center St. Petersburg) in St. Petersburg, Russian Federation.

(D) Zorsecurity (also known as Esage Lab) in Moscow, Russian Federation.

(E) The autonomous noncommercial organization known as the Professional Association of Designers of Data Processing Systems (also known as ANO PO KSI) in Moscow, Russian Federation.

(F) Igor Valentinovich Korobov.

(G) Sergey Aleksandrovich Gizunov.

(H) Igor Olegovich Kostyukov.

(I) Vladimir Stepanovich Alexseyev.

(6) On January 6, 2017, an assessment of the United States intelligence community entitled, "Assessing Russian Activities and Intentions in Recent U.S. Elections" stated, "Russian President Vladimir Putin ordered an influence campaign in 2016 aimed at the United States presidential election." The assessment warns that "Moscow will apply lessons learned from its Putin-ordered campaign aimed at the U.S. Presidential election to future influence efforts worldwide, including against U.S. allies and their election processes".

SEC. 212. SENSE OF CONGRESS.

It is the sense of Congress that the President—

(1) should continue to uphold and seek unity with European and other key partners on sanctions implemented against the Russian Federation, which have been effective and instrumental in countering Russian aggression in Ukraine;

(2) should engage to the fullest extent possible with partner governments with regard to closing loopholes, including the allowance of extended prepayment for the delivery of goods and commodities and other loopholes, in multilateral and unilateral restrictive measures against the Russian Federation, with the aim of maximizing alignment of those measures; and

(3) should increase efforts to vigorously enforce compliance with sanctions in place as of the date of the enactment of this Act with respect to the Russian Federation in response to the crisis in eastern Ukraine, cyber intrusions and attacks, and human rights violators in the Russian Federation.

PART 1—CONGRESSIONAL REVIEW OF SANCTIONS IMPOSED WITH RESPECT TO THE RUSSIAN FEDERATION

SEC. 215. SHORT TITLE.

This part may be cited as the "Russia Sanctions Review Act of 2017".

SEC. 216. CONGRESSIONAL REVIEW OF CERTAIN ACTIONS RELATING TO SANCTIONS IMPOSED WITH RESPECT TO THE RUSSIAN FEDERATION.

(a) SUBMISSION TO CONGRESS OF PROPOSED ACTION.—

(1) IN GENERAL.—Notwithstanding any other provision of law, before taking any action described in paragraph (2), the President shall submit to the appropriate congressional committees and leadership a report that describes the proposed action and the reasons for that action.

(2) ACTIONS DESCRIBED.—

(A) IN GENERAL.—An action described in this paragraph is—

(i) an action to terminate the application of any sanctions described in subparagraph (B);

(ii) with respect to sanctions described in subparagraph (B) imposed by the President with respect to a person, an action to waive the application of those sanctions with respect to that person; or

(iii) a licensing action that significantly alters United States' foreign policy with regard to the Russian Federation.

(B) SANCTIONS DESCRIBED.—The sanctions described in this subparagraph are—

(i) sanctions provided for under—

(I) this title or any provision of law amended by this title, including the Executive orders codified under section 222;

(II) the Support for the Sovereignty, Integrity, Democracy, and Economic Stability of Ukraine Act of 2014 (22 U.S.C. 8901 et seq.); or

(III) the Ukraine Freedom Support Act of 2014 (22 U.S.C. 8921 et seq.); and

(ii) the prohibition on access to the properties of the Government of the Russian Federation located in Maryland and New York that the President ordered vacated on December 29, 2016.

(3) DESCRIPTION OF TYPE OF ACTION.—Each report submitted under paragraph (1) with respect to an action described in paragraph (2) shall include a description of whether the action—

(A) is not intended to significantly alter United States foreign policy with regard to the Russian Federation; or

(B) is intended to significantly alter United States foreign policy with regard to the Russian Federation.

(4) INCLUSION OF ADDITIONAL MATTER.—

(A) IN GENERAL.—Each report submitted under paragraph (1) that relates to an action that is intended to significantly alter United States foreign policy with regard to the Russian Federation shall include a description of—

(i) the significant alteration to United States foreign policy with regard to the Russian Federation;

(ii) the anticipated effect of the action on the national security interests of the United States; and

(iii) the policy objectives for which the sanctions affected by the action were initially imposed.

(B) REQUESTS FROM BANKING AND FINANCIAL SERVICES COMMITTEES.—The Committee on Banking, Housing, and Urban Affairs of the Senate or the Committee on Financial Services of the House of Representatives may request the submission to the Committee of the matter described in clauses (ii) and (iii) of subparagraph (A) with respect to a report submitted under paragraph (1) that relates to an action that is not intended to significantly alter United States foreign policy with regard to the Russian Federation.

(5) CONFIDENTIALITY OF PROPRIETARY INFORMATION.—Proprietary information that can be associated with a particular person with respect to an action described in paragraph (2) may be included in a report submitted under paragraph (1) only if the appropriate congressional committees and leadership provide assurances of confidentiality, unless such person otherwise consents in writing to such disclosure.

(6) RULE OF CONSTRUCTION.—Paragraph (2)(A)(iii) shall not be construed to require the submission of a report under paragraph (1) with respect

to the routine issuance of a license that does not significantly alter United States foreign policy with regard to the Russian Federation.

(b) PERIOD FOR REVIEW BY CONGRESS.—

(1) IN GENERAL.—During the period of 30 calendar days beginning on the date on which the President submits a report under subsection (a)(1)—

(A) in the case of a report that relates to an action that is not intended to significantly alter United States foreign policy with regard to the Russian Federation, the Committee on Banking, Housing, and Urban Affairs of the Senate and the Committee on Financial Services of the House of Representatives should, as appropriate, hold hearings and briefings and otherwise obtain information in order to fully review the report; and

(B) in the case of a report that relates to an action that is intended to significantly alter United States foreign policy with regard to the Russian Federation, the Committee on Foreign Relations of the Senate and the Committee on Foreign Affairs of the House of Representatives should, as appropriate, hold hearings and briefings and otherwise obtain information in order to fully review the report.

(2) EXCEPTION.—The period for congressional review under paragraph (1) of a report required to be submitted under subsection (a)(1) shall be 60 calendar days if the report is submitted on or after July 10 and on or before September 7 in any calendar year.

(3) LIMITATION ON ACTIONS DURING INITIAL CONGRESSIONAL REVIEW PERIOD.— Notwithstanding any other provision of law, during the period for congressional review provided for under paragraph (1) of a report submitted under subsection (a)(1) proposing an action described in subsection (a)(2), including any additional period for such review as applicable under the exception provided in paragraph (2), the President may not take that action unless a joint resolution of approval with respect to that action is enacted in accordance with subsection (c).

(4) LIMITATION ON ACTIONS DURING PRESIDENTIAL CONSIDERATION OF A JOINT RESOLUTION OF DISAPPROVAL.— Notwithstanding any other provision of law, if a joint resolution of disapproval relating to a report submitted under subsection (a)(1) proposing an action described in subsection (a)(2) passes both Houses of Congress in accordance with subsection (c), the President may not take that action for a period of 12 calendar days after the date of passage of the joint resolution of disapproval.

(5) LIMITATION ON ACTIONS DURING CONGRESSIONAL RECONSIDERATION OF A JOINT RESOLUTION OF DISAPPROVAL.— Notwithstanding any other provision of law, if a joint resolution of disapproval relating to a report submitted under subsection (a)(1) proposing an action described in subsection (a)(2) passes both Houses of Congress in accordance with subsection (c), and the President vetoes the joint resolution, the President may not take that action for a period of 10 calendar days after the date of the President's veto.

(6) EFFECT OF ENACTMENT OF A JOINT RESOLUTION OF DISAPPROVAL.— Notwithstanding any other provision of law, if a joint resolution of disapproval relating to a report submitted under subsection (a)(1) proposing an action described in subsection (a)(2) is enacted in accordance with subsection (c), the President may not take that action.

(c) Joint resolutions of disapproval or approval defined.—In this subsection:

(1) JOINT RESOLUTION OF APPROVAL.—The term "joint resolution of approval" means only a joint resolution of either House of Congress—

(A) the title of which is as follows: "A joint resolution approving the President's proposal to take an action relating to the application of certain sanctions with respect to the Russian Federation."; and

(B) the sole matter after the resolving clause of which is the following: "Congress approves of the action relating to the application of sanctions imposed with respect to the Russian Federation proposed by the President in the report submitted to Congress under section 216(a)(1) of the Russia Sanctions Review Act of 2017 on _____ relating to _____.", with the first blank space being filled with the appropriate date and the second blank space being filled with a short description of the proposed action.

(2) JOINT RESOLUTION OF DISAPPROVAL.—The term "joint resolution of disapproval" means only a joint resolution of either House of Congress—

(A) the title of which is as follows: "A joint resolution disapproving the President's proposal to take an action relating to the application of certain sanctions with respect to the Russian Federation."; and

(B) the sole matter after the resolving clause of which is the following: "Congress disapproves of the action relating to the application of sanctions imposed with respect to the Russian Federation proposed by the President in the report submitted to Congress under section 216(a)(1) of the Russia Sanctions Review Act of 2017 on _____ relating to _____.", with the first blank space being filled with the appropriate date and the second blank space being filled with a short description of the proposed action.

(3) INTRODUCTION.—During the period of 30 calendar days provided for under subsection (b)(1), including any additional period as applicable under the exception provided in subsection (b)(2), a joint resolution of approval or joint resolution of disapproval may be introduced—

(A) in the House of Representatives, by the majority leader or the minority leader; and

(B) in the Senate, by the majority leader (or the majority leader's designee) or the minority leader (or the minority leader's designee).

(4) FLOOR CONSIDERATION IN HOUSE OF REPRESENTATIVES.—If a committee of the House of Representatives to which a joint resolution of approval or joint resolution of disapproval has been referred has not reported the joint resolution within 10 calendar days after the date of referral, that committee

shall be discharged from further consideration of the joint resolution.

(5) CONSIDERATION IN THE SENATE.—

(A) COMMITTEE REFERRAL.—A joint resolution of approval or joint resolution of disapproval introduced in the Senate shall be—

(i) referred to the Committee on Banking, Housing, and Urban Affairs if the joint resolution relates to a report under subsection (a)(3)(A) that relates to an action that is not intended to significantly alter United States foreign policy with regard to the Russian Federation; and

(ii) referred to the Committee on Foreign Relations if the joint resolution relates to a report under subsection (a)(3)(B) that relates to an action that is intended to significantly alter United States foreign policy with respect to the Russian Federation.

(B) REPORTING AND DISCHARGE.—If the committee to which a joint resolution of approval or joint resolution of disapproval was referred has not reported the joint resolution within 10 calendar days after the date of referral of the joint resolution, that committee shall be discharged from further consideration of the joint resolution and the joint resolution shall be placed on the appropriate calendar.

(C) PROCEEDING TO CONSIDERATION.— Notwithstanding Rule XXII of the Standing Rules of the Senate, it is in order at any time after the Committee on Banking, Housing, and Urban Affairs or the Committee on Foreign Relations, as the case may be, reports a joint resolution of approval or joint resolution of disapproval to the Senate or has been discharged from consideration of such a joint resolution (even though a previous motion to the same effect has been disagreed to) to move to proceed to the consideration of the joint resolution, and all points of order against the joint resolution (and against consideration of the joint resolution) are waived. The motion to proceed is not debatable. The motion is not subject to a motion to postpone. A motion to reconsider the vote by which the motion is agreed to or disagreed to shall not be in order.

(D) RULINGS OF THE CHAIR ON PROCEDURE.— Appeals from the decisions of the Chair relating to the application of the rules of the Senate, as the case may be, to the procedure relating to a joint resolution of approval or joint resolution of disapproval shall be decided without debate.

(E) CONSIDERATION OF VETO MESSAGES.— Debate in the Senate of any veto message with respect to a joint resolution of approval or joint resolution of disapproval, including all debatable motions and appeals in connection with the joint resolution, shall be limited to 10 hours, to be equally divided between, and controlled by, the majority leader and the minority leader or their designees.

(6) RULES RELATING TO SENATE AND HOUSE OF REPRESENTATIVES.—

(A) TREATMENT OF SENATE JOINT RESOLUTION IN HOUSE.—In the House of

Representatives, the following procedures shall apply to a joint resolution of approval or a joint resolution of disapproval received from the Senate (unless the House has already passed a joint resolution relating to the same proposed action):

(i) The joint resolution shall be referred to the appropriate committees.

(ii) If a committee to which a joint resolution has been referred has not reported the joint resolution within 2 calendar days after the date of referral, that committee shall be discharged from further consideration of the joint resolution.

(iii) Beginning on the third legislative day after each committee to which a joint resolution has been referred reports the joint resolution to the House or has been discharged from further consideration thereof, it shall be in order to move to proceed to consider the joint resolution in the House. All points of order against the motion are waived. Such a motion shall not be in order after the House has disposed of a motion to proceed on the joint resolution. The previous question shall be considered as ordered on the motion to its adoption without intervening motion. The motion shall not be debatable. A motion to reconsider the vote by which the motion is disposed of shall not be in order.

(iv) The joint resolution shall be considered as read. All points of order against the joint resolution and against its consideration are waived. The previous question shall be considered as ordered on the joint resolution to final passage without intervening motion except 2 hours of debate equally divided and controlled by the sponsor of the joint resolution (or a designee) and an opponent. A motion to reconsider the vote on passage of the joint resolution shall not be in order.

(B) TREATMENT OF HOUSE JOINT RESOLUTION IN SENATE.—

(i) If, before the passage by the Senate of a joint resolution of approval or joint resolution of disapproval, the Senate receives an identical joint resolution from the House of Representatives, the following procedures shall apply:

(I) That joint resolution shall not be referred to a committee.

(II) With respect to that joint resolution—

(aa) the procedure in the Senate shall be the same as if no joint resolution had been received from the House of Representatives; but

(bb) the vote on passage shall be on the joint resolution from the House of Representatives.

(ii) If, following passage of a joint resolution of approval or joint resolution of disapproval in the Senate, the Senate receives an identical joint resolution from the House of Representatives, that joint resolution shall be placed on the appropriate Senate calendar.

(iii) If a joint resolution of approval or a joint resolution of disapproval is received from the House, and no companion joint resolution has been introduced in the Senate, the Senate procedures under this subsection shall apply to the House joint resolution.

(C) APPLICATION TO REVENUE MEASURES.—
The provisions of this paragraph shall not apply in the
House of Representatives to a joint resolution of
approval or joint resolution of disapproval that is a
revenue measure.

(7) RULES OF HOUSE OF REPRESENTATIVES
AND SENATE.—This subsection is enacted by
Congress—

(A) as an exercise of the rulemaking power of the
Senate and the House of Representatives, respectively,
and as such is deemed a part of the rules of each House,
respectively, and supersedes other rules only to the
extent that it is inconsistent with such rules; and

(B) with full recognition of the constitutional right of
either House to change the rules (so far as relating to
the procedure of that House) at any time, in the same
manner, and to the same extent as in the case of any
other rule of that House.

(d) Appropriate congressional committees and
leadership defined.—In this section, the term
"appropriate congressional committees and leadership"
means—

(1) the Committee on Banking, Housing, and Urban
Affairs, the Committee on Foreign Relations, and the
majority and minority leaders of the Senate; and

(2) the Committee on Financial Services, the
Committee on Foreign Affairs, and the Speaker, the
majority leader, and the minority leader of the House of
Representatives.

PART 2—SANCTIONS WITH RESPECT TO THE RUSSIAN FEDERATION

SEC. 221. DEFINITIONS.

In this part:

(1) APPROPRIATE CONGRESSIONAL COMMITTEES.—The term "appropriate congressional committees" means—

(A) the Committee on Banking, Housing, and Urban Affairs, the Committee on Foreign Relations, and the Committee on Finance of the Senate; and

(B) the Committee on Foreign Affairs, the Committee on Financial Services, and the Committee on Ways and Means of the House of Representatives.

(2) GOOD.—The term "good" has the meaning given that term in section 16 of the Export Administration Act of 1979 (50 U.S.C. 4618) (as continued in effect pursuant to the International Emergency Economic Powers Act (50 U.S.C. 1701 et seq.)).

(3) INTERNATIONAL FINANCIAL INSTITUTION.—The term "international financial institution" has the meaning given that term in section 1701(c) of the International Financial Institutions Act (22 U.S.C. 262r(c)).

(4) KNOWINGLY.—The term "knowingly", with respect to conduct, a circumstance, or a result, means that a person has actual knowledge, or should have known, of the conduct, the circumstance, or the result.

(5) PERSON.—The term "person" means an individual or entity.

(6) UNITED STATES PERSON.—The term "United States person" means—

(A) a United States citizen or an alien lawfully admitted for permanent residence to the United States; or

(B) an entity organized under the laws of the United States or of any jurisdiction within the United States, including a foreign branch of such an entity.

SEC. 222. **CODIFICATION OF SANCTIONS RELATING TO THE RUSSIAN FEDERATION.**

(a) CODIFICATION.—United States sanctions provided for in Executive Order No. 13660 (79 Fed. Reg. 13493; relating to blocking property of certain persons contributing to the situation in Ukraine), Executive Order No. 13661 (79 Fed. Reg. 15535; relating to blocking property of additional persons contributing to the situation in Ukraine), Executive Order No. 13662 (79 Fed. Reg. 16169; relating to blocking property of additional persons contributing to the situation in Ukraine), Executive Order No. 13685 (79 Fed. Reg. 77357; relating to blocking property of certain persons and prohibiting certain transactions with respect to the Crimea region of Ukraine), Executive Order No. 13694 (80 Fed. Reg. 18077; relating to blocking the property of certain persons engaging in significant malicious cyber-enabled activities), and Executive Order No.

13757 (82 Fed. Reg. 1; relating to taking additional steps to address the national emergency with respect to significant malicious cyber-enabled activities), as in effect on the day before the date of the enactment of this Act, including with respect to all persons sanctioned under such Executive orders, shall remain in effect except as provided in subsection (b).

(b) TERMINATION OF CERTAIN SANCTIONS.—Subject to section 216, the President may terminate the application of sanctions described in subsection (a) that are imposed on a person in connection with activity conducted by the person if the President submits to the appropriate congressional committees a notice that—

(1) the person is not engaging in the activity that was the basis for the sanctions or has taken significant verifiable steps toward stopping the activity; and

(2) the President has received reliable assurances that the person will not knowingly engage in activity subject to sanctions described in subsection (a) in the future.

(c) APPLICATION OF NEW CYBER SANCTIONS.—The President may waive the initial application under subsection (a) of sanctions with respect to a person under Executive Order No. 13694 or 13757 only if the President submits to the appropriate congressional committees—

(1) a written determination that the waiver—

(A) is in the vital national security interests of the United States; or

(B) will further the enforcement of this title; and

(2) a certification that the Government of the Russian Federation has made significant efforts to reduce the number and intensity of cyber intrusions conducted by that Government.

(d) APPLICATION OF NEW UKRAINE-RELATED SANCTIONS.—The President may waive the initial application under subsection (a) of sanctions with respect to a person under Executive Order No. 13660, 13661, 13662, or 13685 only if the President submits to the appropriate congressional committees—

(1) a written determination that the waiver—

(A) is in the vital national security interests of the United States; or

(B) will further the enforcement of this title; and

(2) a certification that the Government of the Russian Federation is taking steps to implement the Minsk Agreement to address the ongoing conflict in eastern Ukraine, signed in Minsk, Belarus, on February 11, 2015, by the leaders of Ukraine, Russia, France, and Germany, the Minsk Protocol, which was agreed to on September 5, 2014, and any successor agreements that are agreed to by the Government of Ukraine.

SEC. 223. MODIFICATION OF IMPLEMENTATION OF EXECUTIVE ORDER NO. 13662.

(a) DETERMINATION THAT CERTAIN ENTITIES ARE SUBJECT TO SANCTIONS.—The Secretary of the Treasury may determine that a person meets one or more of the criteria in section 1(a) of Executive Order No. 13662 if that person is a state-owned entity operating in the railway or metals and mining sector of the economy of the Russian Federation.

(b) MODIFICATION OF DIRECTIVE 1 WITH RESPECT TO THE FINANCIAL SERVICES SECTOR OF THE RUSSIAN FEDERATION ECONOMY.—Not later than 60 days after the date of the enactment of this Act, the Secretary of the Treasury shall modify Directive 1 (as amended), dated September 12, 2014, issued by the Office of Foreign Assets Control under Executive Order No. 13662, or any successor directive (which shall be effective beginning on the date that is 60 days after the date of such modification), to ensure that the directive prohibits the conduct by United States persons or persons within the United States of all transactions in, provision of financing for, and other dealings in new debt of longer than 14 days maturity or new equity of persons determined to be subject to the directive, their property, or their interests in property.

(c) MODIFICATION OF DIRECTIVE 2 WITH RESPECT TO THE ENERGY SECTOR OF THE RUSSIAN FEDERATION ECONOMY.—Not later than 60 days after the date of the enactment of this Act, the Secretary of the Treasury shall modify Directive 2 (as amended), dated September 12, 2014, issued by the Office of Foreign Assets Control under Executive Order No. 13662, or any successor directive (which shall be effective beginning on the date that is 60 days after the date of such modification), to ensure that the directive prohibits the conduct by United States persons or persons within the United States of all transactions in, provision of financing for, and other dealings in new debt of longer than 60 days maturity of persons determined to be subject to the directive, their property, or their interests in property.

(d) MODIFICATION OF DIRECTIVE 4.—Not later than 90 days after the date of the enactment of this Act, the Secretary of the Treasury shall modify Directive 4, dated September 12, 2014, issued by the Office of Foreign Assets Control under Executive Order No. 13662, or any successor directive (which shall be effective beginning on the date that is 90 days after the date of such modification), to ensure that the directive prohibits the provision, exportation, or reexportation, directly or indirectly, by United States persons or persons within the United States, of goods, services (except for financial services), or technology in support of exploration or production for new deepwater, Arctic offshore, or shale projects—

(1) that have the potential to produce oil; and

(2) that involve any person determined to be subject to the directive or the property or interests in property of such a person who has a controlling interest or a substantial non-controlling ownership interest in such a project defined as not less than a 33 percent interest.

SEC. 224. IMPOSITION OF SANCTIONS WITH RESPECT TO ACTIVITIES OF THE RUSSIAN

FEDERATION UNDERMINING CYBER SECURITY.

(a) IN GENERAL.—On and after the date that is 60 days after the date of the enactment of this Act, the President shall—

(1) impose the sanctions described in subsection (b) with respect to any person that the President determines—

(A) knowingly engages in significant activities undermining cybersecurity against any person, including a democratic institution, or government on behalf of the Government of the Russian Federation; or

(B) is owned or controlled by, or acts or purports to act for or on behalf of, directly or indirectly, a person described in subparagraph (A);

(2) impose five or more of the sanctions described in section 235 with respect to any person that the President determines knowingly materially assists, sponsors, or provides financial, material, or technological support for, or goods or services (except financial services) in support of, an activity described in paragraph (1)(A); and

(3) impose three or more of the sanctions described in section 4(c) of the of the Ukraine Freedom Support Act of 2014 (22 U.S.C. 8923(c)) with respect to any person that the President determines knowingly provides financial services in support of an activity described in paragraph (1)(A).

(b) SANCTIONS DESCRIBED.—The sanctions described in this subsection are the following:

(1) ASSET BLOCKING.—The exercise of all powers granted to the President by the International Emergency Economic Powers Act (50 U.S.C. 1701 et seq.) to the extent necessary to block and prohibit all transactions in all property and interests in property of a person determined by the President to be subject to subsection (a)(1) if such property and interests in property are in the United States, come within the United States, or are or come within the possession or control of a United States person.

(2) EXCLUSION FROM THE UNITED STATES AND REVOCATION OF VISA OR OTHER DOCUMENTATION.—In the case of an alien determined by the President to be subject to subsection (a)(1), denial of a visa to, and exclusion from the United States of, the alien, and revocation in accordance with section 221(i) of the Immigration and Nationality Act (8 U.S.C. 1201(i)), of any visa or other documentation of the alien.

(c) APPLICATION OF NEW CYBER SANCTIONS.—The President may waive the initial application under subsection (a) of sanctions with respect to a person only if the President submits to the appropriate congressional committees—

(1) a written determination that the waiver—

(A) is in the vital national security interests of the United States; or

(B) will further the enforcement of this title; and

(2) a certification that the Government of the Russian Federation has made significant efforts to reduce the number and intensity of cyber intrusions conducted by that Government.

(d) SIGNIFICANT ACTIVITIES UNDERMINING CYBER SECURITY DEFINED.—In this section, the term "significant activities undermining cyber security" includes—

(1) significant efforts—

(A) to deny access to or degrade, disrupt, or destroy an information and communications technology system or network; or

(B) to exfiltrate, degrade, corrupt, destroy, or release information from such a system or network without authorization for purposes of—

(i) conducting influence operations; or

(ii) causing a significant misappropriation of funds, economic resources, trade secrets, personal identifications, or financial information for commercial or competitive advantage or private financial gain;

(2) significant destructive malware attacks; and

(3) significant denial of service activities.

SEC. 225   IMPOSITION OF SANCTIONS

RELATING TO SPECIAL RUSSIAN CRUDE OIL PROJECTS.

Section 4(b)(1) of the Ukraine Freedom Support Act of 2014 (22 U.S.C. 8923(b)(1)) is amended by striking "on and after the date that is 45 days after the date of the enactment of this Act, the President may impose" and inserting "on and after the date that is 30 days after the date of the enactment of the Countering Russian Influence in Europe and Eurasia Act of 2017, the President shall impose, unless the President determines that it is not in the national interest of the United States to do so,".

SEC. 226. IMPOSITION OF SANCTIONS WITH RESPECT TO RUSSIAN AND OTHER FOREIGN FINANCIAL INSTITUTIONS.

Section 5 of the Ukraine Freedom Support Act of 2014 (22 U.S.C. 8924) is amended—

(1) in subsection (a)—

(A) by striking "may impose" and inserting "shall impose, unless the President determines that it is not in the national interest of the United States to do so,"; and

(B) by striking "on or after the date of the enactment of this Act" and inserting "on or after the date of the enactment of the Countering Russian Influence in Europe and Eurasia Act of 2017"; and

(2) in subsection (b)—

(A) by striking "may impose" and inserting "shall impose, unless the President determines that it is not in the national interest of the United States to do so,"; and

(B) by striking "on or after the date that is 180 days after the date of the enactment of this Act" and inserting "on or after the date that is 30 days after the date of the enactment of the Countering Russian Influence in Europe and Eurasia Act of 2017".

SEC. 227. MANDATORY IMPOSITION OF SANCTIONS WITH RESPECT TO SIGNIFICANT CORRUPTION IN THE RUSSIAN FEDERATION.

Section 9 of the Sovereignty, Integrity, Democracy, and Economic Stability of Ukraine Act of 2014 (22 U.S.C. 8908(a)) is amended—

(1) in subsection (a)—

(A) in the matter preceding paragraph (1), by striking "is authorized and encouraged to" and inserting "shall"; and

(B) in paragraph (1)—

(i) by striking "President determines is" and inserting "President determines is, on or after the date of the enactment of the Countering Russian Influence in Europe and Eurasia Act of 2017,"; and

(ii) by inserting "or elsewhere" after "in the Russian Federation";

(2) by redesignating subsection (d) as subsection (e);

(3) in subsection (c), by striking "The President" and inserting "except as provided in subsection (d), the President"; and

(4) by inserting after subsection (c) the following:

"(d) APPLICATION OF NEW SANCTIONS.—The President may waive the initial application of sanctions under subsection (b) with respect to a person only if the President submits to the appropriate congressional committees—

"(1) a written determination that the waiver—

"(A) is in the vital national security interests of the United States; or

"(B) will further the enforcement of this Act; and

"(2) a certification that the Government of the Russian Federation is taking steps to implement the Minsk Agreement to address the ongoing conflict in eastern Ukraine, signed in Minsk, Belarus, on February 11, 2015, by the leaders of Ukraine, Russia, France, and Germany, the Minsk Protocol, which was agreed to on September 5, 2014, and any successor agreements that are agreed to by the Government of Ukraine.".

SEC. 228. MANDATORY IMPOSITION OF SANCTIONS WITH RESPECT TO CERTAIN

TRANSACTIONS WITH FOREIGN SANCTIONS EVADERS AND SERIOUS HUMAN RIGHTS ABUSERS IN THE RUSSIAN FEDERATION.

(a) IN GENERAL.—The Support for the Sovereignty, Integrity, Democracy, and Economic Stability of Ukraine Act of 2014 (22 U.S.C. 8901 et seq.) is amended by adding at the end the following:

"SEC. 10. MANDATORY IMPOSITION OF SANCTIONS WITH RESPECT TO CERTAIN TRANSACTIONS WITH PERSONS THAT EVADE SANCTIONS IMPOSED WITH RESPECT TO THE RUSSIAN FEDERATION.

"(a) IN GENERAL.—The President shall impose the sanctions described in subsection (b) with respect to a foreign person if the President determines that the foreign person knowingly, on or after the date of the enactment of the Countering Russian Influence in Europe and Eurasia Act of 2017—

"(1) materially violates, attempts to violate, conspires to violate, or causes a violation of any license, order, regulation, or prohibition contained in or issued pursuant to any covered Executive order, this Act, or the Ukraine Freedom Support Act of 2014 (22 U.S.C. 8921 et seq.); or

"(2) facilitates a significant transaction or transactions, including deceptive or structured transactions, for or on behalf of—

"(A) any person subject to sanctions imposed by the

United States with respect to the Russian Federation; or

"(B) any child, spouse, parent, or sibling of an individual described in subparagraph (A).

"(b) SANCTIONS DESCRIBED.—The sanctions described in this subsection are the exercise of all powers granted to the President by the International Emergency Economic Powers Act (50 U.S.C. 1701 et seq.) to the extent necessary to block and prohibit all transactions in all property and interests in property of a person determined by the President to be subject to subsection (a) if such property and interests in property are in the United States, come within the United States, or are or come within the possession or control of a United States person.

"(c) IMPLEMENTATION; PENALTIES.—

"(1) IMPLEMENTATION.—The President may exercise all authorities provided to the President under sections 203 and 205 of the International Emergency Economic Powers Act (50 U.S.C. 1702 and 1704) to carry out subsection (b).

"(2) PENALTIES.—A person that violates, attempts to violate, conspires to violate, or causes a violation of subsection (b) or any regulation, license, or order issued to carry out subsection (b) shall be subject to the penalties set forth in subsections (b) and (c) of section 206 of the International Emergency Economic Powers Act (50 U.S.C. 1705) to the same extent as a person that commits an unlawful act described in subsection (a) of that section.

"(d) APPLICATION OF NEW SANCTIONS.—The President may waive the initial application of sanctions under subsection (b) with respect to a person only if the President submits to the appropriate congressional committees—

"(1) a written determination that the waiver—

"(A) is in the vital national security interests of the United States; or

"(B) will further the enforcement of this Act;

"(2) in the case of sanctions imposed under this section in connection with a covered Executive order described in subparagraph (A), (B), (C), or (D) of subsection (f)(1), a certification that the Government of the Russian Federation is taking steps to implement the Minsk Agreement to address the ongoing conflict in eastern Ukraine, signed in Minsk, Belarus, on February 11, 2015, by the leaders of Ukraine, Russia, France, and Germany, the Minsk Protocol, which was agreed to on September 5, 2014, and any successor agreements that are agreed to by the Government of Ukraine; and

"(3) in the case of sanctions imposed under this section in connection with a covered Executive order described in subparagraphs (E) or (F) of subsection (f)(1), a certification that the Government of the Russian Federation has made significant efforts to reduce the number and intensity of cyber intrusions conducted by that Government.

"(e) TERMINATION.—Subject to section 216 of the

Russia Sanctions Review Act of 2017, the President may terminate the application of sanctions under subsection (b) with respect to a person if the President submits to the appropriate congressional committees—

"(1) a notice of and justification for the termination; and

"(2) a notice that—

"(A) the person is not engaging in the activity that was the basis for the sanctions or has taken significant verifiable steps toward stopping the activity; and

"(B) the President has received reliable assurances that the person will not knowingly engage in activity subject to sanctions under subsection (a) in the future.

"(f) DEFINITIONS.—In this section:

"(1) COVERED EXECUTIVE ORDER.—The term 'covered Executive order' means any of the following:

"(A) Executive Order No. 13660 (79 Fed. Reg. 13493; relating to blocking property of certain persons contributing to the situation in Ukraine).

"(B) Executive Order No. 13661 (79 Fed. Reg. 15535; relating to blocking property of additional persons contributing to the situation in Ukraine).

"(C) Executive Order No. 13662 (79 Fed. Reg. 16169; relating to blocking property of additional persons contributing to the situation in Ukraine).

"(D) Executive Order No. 13685 (79 Fed. Reg. 77357;

relating to blocking property of certain persons and prohibiting certain transactions with respect to the Crimea region of Ukraine).

"(E) Executive Order No. 13694 (80 Fed. Reg. 18077; relating to blocking the property of certain persons engaging in significant malicious cyber-enabled activities), relating to the Russian Federation.

"(F) Executive Order No. 13757 (82 Fed. Reg. 1; relating to taking additional steps to address the national emergency with respect to significant malicious cyber-enabled activities), relating to the Russian Federation.

"(2) FOREIGN PERSON.—The term 'foreign person' has the meaning given such term in section 595.304 of title 31, Code of Federal Regulations (as in effect on the date of the enactment of this section).

"(3) STRUCTURED.—The term 'structured', with respect to a transaction, has the meaning given the term 'structure' in paragraph (xx) of section 1010.100 of title 31, Code of Federal Regulations (or any corresponding similar regulation or ruling).

"SEC. 11. MANDATORY IMPOSITION OF SANCTIONS WITH RESPECT TO TRANSACTIONS WITH PERSONS RESPONSIBLE FOR HUMAN RIGHTS ABUSES.

"(a) IN GENERAL.—The President shall impose the sanctions described in subsection (b) with respect to a foreign person if the President determines that the foreign person, based on credible information, on or after the date of the enactment of this section—

"(1) is responsible for, complicit in, or responsible for ordering, controlling, or otherwise directing, the commission of serious human rights abuses in any territory forcibly occupied or otherwise controlled by the Government of the Russian Federation;

"(2) materially assists, sponsors, or provides financial, material, or technological support for, or goods or services to, a foreign person described in paragraph (1); or

"(3) is owned or controlled by, or acts or purports to act for or on behalf of, directly or indirectly, a foreign person described in paragraph (1).

"(b) SANCTIONS DESCRIBED.—

"(1) ASSET BLOCKING.—The exercise of all powers granted to the President by the International Emergency Economic Powers Act (50 U.S.C. 1701 et seq.) to the extent necessary to block and prohibit all transactions in all property and interests in property of a person determined by the President to be subject to subsection (a) if such property and interests in property are in the United States, come within the United States, or are or come within the possession or control of a United States person.

"(2) EXCLUSION FROM THE UNITED STATES AND REVOCATION OF VISA OR OTHER DOCUMENTATION.—In the case of an alien determined by the President to be subject to subsection (a), denial of a visa to, and exclusion from the United

States of, the alien, and revocation in accordance with section 221(i) of the Immigration and Nationality Act (8 U.S.C. 1201(i)), of any visa or other documentation of the alien.

"(c) APPLICATION OF NEW SANCTIONS.—The President may waive the initial application of sanctions under subsection (b) with respect to a person only if the President submits to the appropriate congressional committees—

"(1) a written determination that the waiver—

"(A) is in the vital national security interests of the United States; or

"(B) will further the enforcement of this Act; and

"(2) a certification that the Government of the Russian Federation has made efforts to reduce serious human rights abuses in territory forcibly occupied or otherwise controlled by that Government.

"(d) IMPLEMENTATION; PENALTIES.—

"(1) **IMPLEMENTATION**.—The President may exercise all authorities provided to the President under sections 203 and 205 of the International Emergency Economic Powers Act (50 U.S.C. 1702 and 1704) to carry out subsection (b)(1).

"(2) PENALTIES.—A person that violates, attempts to violate, conspires to violate, or causes a violation of subsection (b)(1) or any regulation, license, or order issued to carry out subsection (b)(1) shall be subject to the penalties set forth in subsections (b) and (c) of section 206 of the International Emergency Economic Powers Act (50 U.S.C. 1705) to the same extent as a person that commits an unlawful act described in subsection (a) of that section.

"(e) TERMINATION.—Subject to section 216 of Russia Sanctions Review Act of 2017, the President may terminate the application of sanctions under subsection (b) with respect to a person if the President submits to the appropriate congressional committees—

"(1) a notice of and justification for the termination; and

"(2) a notice—

"(A) that—

"(i) the person is not engaging in the activity that was the basis for the sanctions or has taken significant verifiable steps toward stopping the activity; and

"(ii) the President has received reliable assurances that the person will not knowingly engage in activity subject to sanctions under subsection (a) in the future; or

"(B) that the President determines that insufficient basis exists for the determination by the President under subsection (a) with respect to the person.".

(b) DEFINITION OF APPROPRIATE CONGRESSIONAL COMMITTEES.—Section 2(2) of the Support for the Sovereignty, Integrity, Democracy, and Economic Stability of Ukraine Act of 2014 (22 U.S.C. 8901(2)) is amended—

(1) in subparagraph (A), by inserting "the Committee on Banking, Housing, and Urban Affairs," before "the Committee on Foreign Relations"; and

(2) in subparagraph (B), by inserting "the Committee on Financial Services" before "the Committee on Foreign Affairs".

SEC. 229. NOTIFICATIONS TO CONGRESS UNDER UKRAINE FREEDOM SUPPORT ACT OF 2014.

(a) SANCTIONS RELATING TO DEFENSE AND ENERGY SECTORS OF THE RUSSIAN FEDERATION.—Section 4 of the Ukraine Freedom Support Act of 2014 (22 U.S.C. 8923) is amended—

(1) by redesignating subsections (g) and (h) as subsections (h) and (i), respectively;

(2) by inserting after subsection (f) the following:

"(g) NOTIFICATIONS AND CERTIFICATIONS TO CONGRESS.—

"(1) IMPOSITION OF SANCTIONS.—The President

shall notify the appropriate congressional committees in writing not later than 15 days after imposing sanctions with respect to a foreign person under subsection (a) or (b).

"(2) TERMINATION OF SANCTIONS WITH RESPECT TO RUSSIAN PRODUCERS, TRANSFERORS, OR BROKERS OF DEFENSE ARTICLES.—Subject to section 216 of the Russia Sanctions Review Act of 2017, the President may terminate the imposition of sanctions under subsection (a)(2) with respect to a foreign person if the President submits to the appropriate congressional committees—

"(A) a notice of and justification for the termination; and

"(B) a notice that—

"(i) the foreign person is not engaging in the activity that was the basis for the sanctions or has taken significant verifiable steps toward stopping the activity; and

"(ii) the President has received reliable assurances that the foreign person will not knowingly engage in activity subject to sanctions under subsection (a)(2) in the future."; and

(3) in subparagraph (B)(ii) of subsection (a)(3), by striking "subsection (h)" and inserting "subsection (i)".

(b) Sanctions on Russian and other foreign financial institutions.—Section 5 of the Ukraine Freedom Support Act of 2014 (22 U.S.C. 8924) is amended—

(1) by redesignating subsections (e) and (f) as subsections (f) and (g), respectively;

(2) by inserting after subsection (d) the following:

"(e) Notification to Congress on imposition of sanctions.—The President shall notify the appropriate congressional committees in writing not later than 15 days after imposing sanctions with respect to a foreign financial institution under subsection (a) or (b).''; and

(3) in subsection (g), as redesignated by paragraph (1), by striking "section 4(h)" and inserting "section 4(i)".

SEC. 230. STANDARDS FOR TERMINATION OF CERTAIN SANCTIONS WITH RESPECT TO THE RUSSIAN FEDERATION.

(a) SANCTIONS RELATING TO UNDERMINING THE PEACE, SECURITY, STABILITY, SOVEREIGNTY, OR TERRITORIAL INTEGRITY OF UKRAINE.—Section 8 of the Sovereignty, Integrity, Democracy, and Economic Stability of Ukraine Act of 2014 (22 U.S.C. 8907) is amended—

(1) by redesignating subsection (d) as subsection (e); and

(2) by inserting after subsection (c) the following:

"(d) TERMINATION.—Subject to section 216 of the Russia Sanctions Review Act of 2017, the President may terminate the application of sanctions under subsection (b) with respect to a person if the President submits to the appropriate congressional committees a notice that—

"(1) the person is not engaging in the activity that was the basis for the sanctions or has taken significant verifiable steps toward stopping the activity; and

"(2) the President has received reliable assurances that the person will not knowingly engage in activity subject to sanctions under subsection (a) in the future.".

(b) SANCTIONS RELATING TO CORRUPTION.—Section 9 of the Sovereignty, Integrity, Democracy, and Economic Stability of Ukraine Act of 2014 (22 U.S.C. 8908) is amended—

(1) by redesignating subsection (d) as subsection (e); and

(2) by inserting after subsection (c) the following:

"(d) TERMINATION.—Subject to section 216 of the Russia Sanctions Review Act of 2017, the President may terminate the application of sanctions under subsection (b) with respect to a person if the President submits to the appropriate congressional committees a notice that—

"(1) the person is not engaging in the activity that was the basis for the sanctions or has taken significant verifiable steps toward stopping the activity; and

"(2) the President has received reliable assurances that the person will not knowingly engage in activity subject to sanctions under subsection (a) in the future.".

SEC. 231. IMPOSITION OF SANCTIONS WITH RESPECT TO PERSONS ENGAGING IN TRANSACTIONS WITH THE INTELLIGENCE OR DEFENSE SECTORS OF THE GOVERNMENT OF THE RUSSIAN FEDERATION.

(a) IN GENERAL.—On and after the date that is 180 days after the date of the enactment of this Act, the President shall impose five or more of the sanctions described in section 235 with respect to a person the President determines knowingly, on or after such date of enactment, engages in a significant transaction with a person that is part of, or operates for or on behalf of, the defense or intelligence sectors of the Government of the Russian Federation, including the Main Intelligence Agency of the General Staff of the Armed Forces of the Russian Federation or the Federal Security Service of the Russian Federation.

(b) APPLICATION OF NEW SANCTIONS.—The President may waive the initial application of sanctions under subsection (a) with respect to a person only if the President submits to the appropriate congressional committees—

(1) a written determination that the waiver—

(A) is in the vital national security interests of the United States; or

(B) will further the enforcement of this title; and

(2) a certification that the Government of the Russian Federation has made significant efforts to reduce the

number and intensity of cyber intrusions conducted by that Government.

(c) DELAY OF IMPOSITION OF SANCTIONS.—The President may delay the imposition of sanctions under subsection (a) with respect to a person if the President certifies to the appropriate congressional committees, not less frequently than every 180 days while the delay is in effect, that the person is substantially reducing the number of significant transactions described in subsection (a) in which that person engages.

(d) REQUIREMENT TO ISSUE GUIDANCE.—Not later than 60 days after the date of the enactment of this Act, the President shall issue regulations or other guidance to specify the persons that are part of, or operate for or on behalf of, the defense and intelligence sectors of the Government of the Russian Federation.

(e) PENALTIES.—A person that violates, attempts to violate, conspires to violate, or causes a violation of subsection (a) or any regulation, license, or order issued to carry out subsection (a) shall be subject to the penalties set forth in subsections (b) and (c) of section 206 of the International Emergency Economic Powers Act (50 U.S.C. 1705) to the same extent as a person that commits an unlawful act described in subsection (a) of that section.

SEC. 232. SANCTIONS WITH RESPECT TO THE DEVELOPMENT OF PIPELINES IN THE RUSSIAN FEDERATION.

(a) IN GENERAL.—The President, in coordination with

allies of the United States, may impose five or more of the sanctions described in section 235 with respect to a person if the President determines that the person knowingly, on or after the date of the enactment of this Act, makes an investment described in subsection (b) or sells, leases, or provides to the Russian Federation, for the construction of Russian energy export pipelines, goods, services, technology, information, or support described in subsection (c)—

(1) any of which has a fair market value of $1,000,000 or more; or

(2) that, during a 12-month period, have an aggregate fair market value of $5,000,000 or more.

(b) INVESTMENT DESCRIBED.—An investment described in this subsection is an investment that directly and significantly contributes to the enhancement of the ability of the Russian Federation to construct energy export pipelines.

(c) GOODS, SERVICES, TECHNOLOGY, INFORMATION, OR SUPPORT DESCRIBED.—Goods, services, technology, information, or support described in this subsection are goods, services, technology, information, or support that could directly and significantly facilitate the maintenance or expansion of the construction, modernization, or repair of energy export pipelines by the Russian Federation.

SEC. 233. SANCTIONS WITH RESPECT TO INVESTMENT IN OR FACILITATION OF PRIVATIZATION OF STATE-OWNED ASSETS

BY THE RUSSIAN FEDERATION.

(a) IN GENERAL.—The President shall impose five or more of the sanctions described in section 235 if the President determines that a person, with actual knowledge, on or after the date of the enactment of this Act, makes an investment of $10,000,000 or more (or any combination of investments of not less than $1,000,000 each, which in the aggregate equals or exceeds $10,000,000 in any 12-month period), or facilitates such an investment, if the investment directly and significantly contributes to the ability of the Russian Federation to privatize state-owned assets in a manner that unjustly benefits—

(1) officials of the Government of the Russian Federation; or

(2) close associates or family members of those officials.

(b) APPLICATION OF NEW SANCTIONS.—The President may waive the initial application of sanctions under subsection (a) with respect to a person only if the President submits to the appropriate congressional committees—

(1) a written determination that the waiver—

(A) is in the vital national security interests of the United States; or

(B) will further the enforcement of this title; and

(2) a certification that the Government of the Russian Federation is taking steps to implement the Minsk

Agreement to address the ongoing conflict in eastern Ukraine, signed in Minsk, Belarus, on February 11, 2015, by the leaders of Ukraine, Russia, France, and Germany, the Minsk Protocol, which was agreed to on September 5, 2014, and any successor agreements that are agreed to by the Government of Ukraine.

SEC. 234. SANCTIONS WITH RESPECT TO THE TRANSFER OF ARMS AND RELATED MATERIEL TO SYRIA.

(a) IMPOSITION OF SANCTIONS.—

(1) IN GENERAL.—The President shall impose on a foreign person the sanctions described in subsection (b) if the President determines that such foreign person has, on or after the date of the enactment of this Act, knowingly exported, transferred, or otherwise provided to Syria significant financial, material, or technological support that contributes materially to the ability of the Government of Syria to—

(A) acquire or develop chemical, biological, or nuclear weapons or related technologies;

(B) acquire or develop ballistic or cruise missile capabilities;

(C) acquire or develop destabilizing numbers and types of advanced conventional weapons;

(D) acquire significant defense articles, defense services, or defense information (as such terms are defined under the Arms Export Control Act (22 U.S.C. 2751 et seq.)); or

(E) acquire items designated by the President for purposes of the United States Munitions List under section 38(a)(1) of the Arms Export Control Act (22 U.S.C. 2778(a)(1)).

(2) APPLICABILITY TO OTHER FOREIGN PERSONS.—The sanctions described in subsection (b) shall also be imposed on any foreign person that—

(A) is a successor entity to a foreign person described in paragraph (1); or

(B) is owned or controlled by, or has acted for or on behalf of, a foreign person described in paragraph (1).

(b) SANCTIONS DESCRIBED.—The sanctions to be imposed on a foreign person described in subsection (a) are the following:

(1) BLOCKING OF PROPERTY.—The President shall exercise all powers granted by the International Emergency Economic Powers Act (50 U.S.C. 1701 et seq.) (except that the requirements of section 202 of such Act (50 U.S.C. 1701) shall not apply) to the extent necessary to block and prohibit all transactions in all property and interests in property of the foreign person if such property and interests in property are in the United States, come within the United States, or are or come within the possession or control of a United States person.

(2) ALIENS INELIGIBLE FOR VISAS, ADMISSION, OR PAROLE.—

(A) EXCLUSION FROM THE UNITED STATES.—

If the foreign person is an individual, the Secretary of State shall deny a visa to, and the Secretary of Homeland Security shall exclude from the United States, the foreign person.

(B) CURRENT VISAS REVOKED.—

(i) IN GENERAL.—The issuing consular officer, the Secretary of State, or the Secretary of Homeland Security (or a designee of one of such Secretaries) shall revoke any visa or other entry documentation issued to the foreign person regardless of when issued.

(ii) EFFECT OF REVOCATION.—A revocation under clause (i) shall take effect immediately and shall automatically cancel any other valid visa or entry documentation that is in the possession of the foreign person.

(c) WAIVER.—Subject to section 216, the President may waive the application of sanctions under subsection (b) with respect to a person if the President determines that such a waiver is in the national security interest of the United States.

(d) DEFINITIONS.—In this section:

(1) FINANCIAL, MATERIAL, OR TECHNOLOGICAL SUPPORT.—The term "financial, material, or technological support" has the meaning given such term in section 542.304 of title 31, Code of Federal Regulations (or any corresponding similar regulation or ruling).

(2) FOREIGN PERSON.—The term "foreign person"

has the meaning given such term in section 594.304 of title 31, Code of Federal Regulations (or any corresponding similar regulation or ruling).

(3) SYRIA.—The term "Syria" has the meaning given such term in section 542.316 of title 31, Code of Federal Regulations (or any corresponding similar regulation or ruling).

SEC. 235. SANCTIONS DESCRIBED.

(a) SANCTIONS DESCRIBED.—The sanctions to be imposed with respect to a person under section 224(a)(2), 231(b), 232(a), or 233(a) are the following:

(1) EXPORT-IMPORT BANK ASSISTANCE FOR EXPORTS TO SANCTIONED PERSONS.—The President may direct the Export-Import Bank of the United States not to give approval to the issuance of any guarantee, insurance, extension of credit, or participation in the extension of credit in connection with the export of any goods or services to the sanctioned person.

(2) EXPORT SANCTION.—The President may order the United States Government not to issue any specific license and not to grant any other specific permission or authority to export any goods or technology to the sanctioned person under—

(A) the Export Administration Act of 1979 (50 U.S.C. 4601 et seq.) (as continued in effect pursuant to the International Emergency Economic Powers Act (50 U.S.C. 1701 et seq.));

(B) the Arms Export Control Act (22 U.S.C. 2751 et seq.);

(C) the Atomic Energy Act of 1954 (42 U.S.C. 2011 et seq.); or

(D) any other statute that requires the prior review and approval of the United States Government as a condition for the export or reexport of goods or services.

(3) LOANS FROM UNITED STATES FINANCIAL INSTITUTIONS.—The President may prohibit any United States financial institution from making loans or providing credits to the sanctioned person totaling more than $10,000,000 in any 12-month period unless the person is engaged in activities to relieve human suffering and the loans or credits are provided for such activities.

(4) LOANS FROM INTERNATIONAL FINANCIAL INSTITUTIONS.—The President may direct the United States executive director to each international financial institution to use the voice and vote of the United States to oppose any loan from the international financial institution that would benefit the sanctioned person.

(5) PROHIBITIONS ON FINANCIAL INSTITUTIONS.—The following prohibitions may be imposed against the sanctioned person if that person is a financial institution:

(A) PROHIBITION ON DESIGNATION AS PRIMARY DEALER.—Neither the Board of Governors of the Federal Reserve System nor the Federal Reserve Bank of New York may designate, or permit the continuation of any prior designation of, the financial institution as a primary dealer in United States Government debt instruments.

(B) PROHIBITION ON SERVICE AS A REPOSITORY OF GOVERNMENT FUNDS.—The financial institution may not serve as agent of the United States Government or serve as repository for United States Government funds.

The imposition of either sanction under subparagraph (A) or (B) shall be treated as one sanction for purposes of subsection (b), and the imposition of both such sanctions shall be treated as two sanctions for purposes of subsection (b).

(6) PROCUREMENT SANCTION.—The United States Government may not procure, or enter into any contract for the procurement of, any goods or services from the sanctioned person.

(7) FOREIGN EXCHANGE.—The President may, pursuant to such regulations as the President may prescribe, prohibit any transactions in foreign exchange that are subject to the jurisdiction of the United States and in which the sanctioned person has any interest.

(8) BANKING TRANSACTIONS.—The President may, pursuant to such regulations as the President may prescribe, prohibit any transfers of credit or payments between financial institutions or by, through, or to any

financial institution, to the extent that such transfers or payments are subject to the jurisdiction of the United States and involve any interest of the sanctioned person.

(9) PROPERTY TRANSACTIONS.—The President may, pursuant to such regulations as the President may prescribe, prohibit any person from—

(A) acquiring, holding, withholding, using, transferring, withdrawing, transporting, importing, or exporting any property that is subject to the jurisdiction of the United States and with respect to which the sanctioned person has any interest;

(B) dealing in or exercising any right, power, or privilege with respect to such property; or

(C) conducting any transaction involving such property.

(10) BAN ON INVESTMENT IN EQUITY OR DEBT OF SANCTIONED PERSON.—The President may, pursuant to such regulations or guidelines as the President may prescribe, prohibit any United States person from investing in or purchasing significant amounts of equity or debt instruments of the sanctioned person.

(11) EXCLUSION OF CORPORATE OFFICERS.— The President may direct the Secretary of State to deny a visa to, and the Secretary of Homeland Security to exclude from the United States, any alien that the President determines is a corporate officer or principal of, or a shareholder with a controlling interest in, the

sanctioned person.

(12) SANCTIONS ON PRINCIPAL EXECUTIVE OFFICERS.—The President may impose on the principal executive officer or officers of the sanctioned person, or on persons performing similar functions and with similar authorities as such officer or officers, any of the sanctions under this subsection.

(b) SANCTIONED PERSON DEFINED.—In this section, the term "sanctioned person" means a person subject to sanctions under section 224(a)(2), 231(b), 232(a), or 233(a).

SEC. 236. EXCEPTIONS, WAIVER, AND TERMINATION.

(a) EXCEPTIONS.—The provisions of this part and amendments made by this part shall not apply with respect to the following:

(1) Activities subject to the reporting requirements under title V of the National Security Act of 1947 (50 U.S.C. 3091 et seq.), or any authorized intelligence activities of the United States.

(2) The admission of an alien to the United States if such admission is necessary to comply with United States obligations under the Agreement between the United Nations and the United States of America regarding the Headquarters of the United Nations, signed at Lake Success June 26, 1947, and entered into force November 21, 1947, under the Convention on Consular Relations, done at Vienna April 24, 1963, and entered into force March 19, 1967, or under other international agreements.

(b) WAIVER OF SANCTIONS THAT ARE IMPOSED.—Subject to section 216, if the President imposes sanctions with respect to a person under this part or the amendments made by this part, the President may waive the application of those sanctions if the President determines that such a waiver is in the national security interest of the United States.

(c) TERMINATION.—Subject to section 216, the President may terminate the application of sanctions under section 224, 231, 232, 233, or 234 with respect to a person if the President submits to the appropriate congressional committees—

(1) a notice of and justification for the termination; and

(2) a notice that—

(A) the person is not engaging in the activity that was the basis for the sanctions or has taken significant verifiable steps toward stopping the activity; and

(B) the President has received reliable assurances that the person will not knowingly engage in activity subject to sanctions under this part in the future.

SEC. 237. EXCEPTION RELATING TO ACTIVITIES OF THE NATIONAL AERONAUTICS AND SPACE ADMINISTRATION.

(a) IN GENERAL.—This Act and the amendments made by this Act shall not apply with respect to activities of the National Aeronautics and Space Administration.

(b) RULE OF CONSTRUCTION.—Nothing in this Act or

the amendments made by this Act shall be construed to authorize the imposition of any sanction or other condition, limitation, restriction, or prohibition, that directly or indirectly impedes the supply by any entity of the Russian Federation of any product or service, or the procurement of such product or service by any contractor or subcontractor of the United States or any other entity, relating to or in connection with any space launch conducted for—

(1) the National Aeronautics and Space Administration; or

(2) any other non-Department of Defense customer.

SEC. 238. RULE OF CONSTRUCTION.

Nothing in this part or the amendments made by this part shall be construed—

(1) to supersede the limitations or exceptions on the use of rocket engines for national security purposes under section 1608 of the Carl Levin and Howard P. "Buck" McKeon National Defense Authorization Act for Fiscal Year 2015 (Public Law 113–291; 128 Stat. 3626; 10 U.S.C. 2271 note), as amended by section 1607 of the National Defense Authorization Act for Fiscal Year 2016 (Public Law 114–92; 129 Stat. 1100) and section 1602 of the National Defense Authorization Act for Fiscal Year 2017 (Public Law 114–328; 130 Stat. 2582); or

(2) to prohibit a contractor or subcontractor of the

Department of Defense from acquiring components referred to in such section 1608.

PART 3—REPORTS

SEC. 241. REPORT ON OLIGARCHS AND PARASTATAL ENTITIES OF THE RUSSIAN FEDERATION.

(a) In general.—Not later than 180 days after the date of the enactment of this Act, the Secretary of the Treasury, in consultation with the Director of National Intelligence and the Secretary of State, shall submit to the appropriate congressional committees a detailed report on the following:

(1) Senior foreign political figures and oligarchs in the Russian Federation, including the following:

(A) An identification of the most significant senior foreign political figures and oligarchs in the Russian Federation, as determined by their closeness to the Russian regime and their net worth.

(B) An assessment of the relationship between individuals identified under subparagraph (A) and President Vladimir Putin or other members of the Russian ruling elite.

(C) An identification of any indices of corruption with respect to those individuals.

(D) The estimated net worth and known sources of income of those individuals and their family members (including spouses, children, parents, and siblings), including assets, investments, other business interests, and relevant beneficial ownership information.

(E) An identification of the non-Russian business affiliations of those individuals.

(2) Russian parastatal entities, including an assessment of the following:

(A) The emergence of Russian parastatal entities and their role in the economy of the Russian Federation.

(B) The leadership structures and beneficial ownership of those entities.

(C) The scope of the non-Russian business affiliations of those entities.

(3) The exposure of key economic sectors of the United States to Russian politically exposed persons and parastatal entities, including, at a minimum, the banking, securities, insurance, and real estate sectors.

(4) The likely effects of imposing debt and equity restrictions on Russian parastatal entities, as well as the anticipated effects of adding Russian parastatal entities to the list of specially designated nationals and blocked persons maintained by the Office of Foreign Assets Control of the Department of the Treasury.

(5) The potential impacts of imposing secondary sanctions with respect to Russian oligarchs, Russian state-owned enterprises, and Russian parastatal entities, including impacts on the entities themselves and on the economy of the Russian Federation, as well as on the economies of the United States and allies of the United

States.

(b) Form of report.—The report required under subsection (a) shall be submitted in an unclassified form, but may contain a classified annex.

(c) Definitions.—In this section:

(1) APPROPRIATE CONGRESSIONAL COMMITTEES.—The term "appropriate congressional committees" means—

(A) the Committee on Banking, Housing, and Urban Affairs, the Committee on Foreign Relations, and the Committee on Finance of the Senate; and

(B) the Committee on Foreign Affairs, the Committee on Financial Services, and the Committee on Ways and Means of the House of Representatives.

(2) SENIOR FOREIGN POLITICAL FIGURE.—The term "senior foreign political figure" has the meaning given that term in section 1010.605 of title 31, Code of Federal Regulations (or any corresponding similar regulation or ruling).

SEC. 242. REPORT ON EFFECTS OF EXPANDING SANCTIONS TO INCLUDE SOVEREIGN DEBT AND DERIVATIVE PRODUCTS.

(a) IN GENERAL.—Not later than 180 days after the date of the enactment of this Act, the Secretary of the Treasury, in consultation with the Director of National Intelligence and the Secretary of State, shall submit to the appropriate congressional committees a report describing in detail the potential effects of expanding sanctions under Directive 1 (as amended), dated September 12, 2014, issued by the Office of Foreign Assets Control under Executive Order No. 13662 (79 Fed. Reg. 16169; relating to blocking property of additional persons contributing to the situation in Ukraine), or any successor directive, to include sovereign debt and the full range of derivative products.

(b) FORM OF REPORT.—The report required under subsection (a) shall be submitted in an unclassified form, but may contain a classified annex.

(c) APPROPRIATE CONGRESSIONAL COMMITTEES DEFINED.—In this section, the term "appropriate congressional committees" means—

(1) the Committee on Banking, Housing, and Urban Affairs, the Committee on Foreign Relations, and the Committee on Finance of the Senate; and

(2) the Committee on Foreign Affairs, the Committee on Financial Services, and the Committee on Ways and Means of the House of Representatives.

SEC. 243. REPORT ON ILLICIT FINANCE RELATING TO THE RUSSIAN FEDERATION.

(a) IN GENERAL.—Not later than 1 year after the date of the enactment of this Act, and not later than the end of each 1-year period thereafter until 2021, the Secretary of the Treasury shall submit to the appropriate congressional committees a report describing interagency efforts in the United States to combat illicit finance relating to the Russian Federation.

(b) ELEMENTS.—The report required by subsection (a) shall contain a summary of efforts by the United States to do the following:

(1) Identify, investigate, map, and disrupt illicit financial flows linked to the Russian Federation if such flows affect the United States financial system or those of major allies of the United States.

(2) Conduct outreach to the private sector, including information sharing efforts to strengthen compliance efforts by entities, including financial institutions, to prevent illicit financial flows described in paragraph (1).

(3) Engage and coordinate with allied international partners on illicit finance, especially in Europe, to coordinate efforts to uncover and prosecute the networks responsible for illicit financial flows described in paragraph (1), including examples of that engagement and coordination.

(4) Identify foreign sanctions evaders and loopholes within the sanctions regimes of foreign partners of the United States.

(5) Expand the number of real estate geographic

targeting orders or other regulatory actions, as appropriate, to degrade illicit financial activity relating to the Russian Federation in relation to the financial system of the United States.

(6) Provide support to counter those involved in illicit finance relating to the Russian Federation across all appropriate law enforcement, intelligence, regulatory, and financial authorities of the Federal Government, including by imposing sanctions with respect to or prosecuting those involved.

(7) In the case of the Department of the Treasury and the Department of Justice, investigate or otherwise develop major cases, including a description of those cases.

(c) BRIEFING.—After submitting a report under this section, the Secretary of the Treasury shall provide briefings to the appropriate congressional committees with respect to that report.

(d) COORDINATION.—The Secretary of the Treasury shall coordinate with the Attorney General, the Director of National Intelligence, the Secretary of Homeland Security, and the Secretary of State in preparing each report under this section.

(e) FORM.—Each report submitted under this section shall be submitted in unclassified form, but may contain a classified annex.

(f) DEFINITIONS.—In this section:

(1)   APPROPRIATE   CONGRESSIONAL COMMITTEES.—The   term   "appropriate

congressional committees" means—

(A) the Committee on Banking, Housing, and Urban Affairs, the Committee on Foreign Relations, and the Committee on Finance of the Senate; and

(B) the Committee on Foreign Affairs, the Committee on Financial Services, and the Committee on Ways and Means of the House of Representatives.

(2) ILLICIT FINANCE.—The term "illicit finance" means the financing of terrorism, narcotics trafficking, or proliferation, money laundering, or other forms of illicit financing domestically or internationally, as defined by the President.

SUBTITLE B—COUNTERING RUSSIAN INFLUENCE IN EUROPE AND EURASIA

SEC. 251. FINDINGS.

Congress makes the following findings:

(1) The Government of the Russian Federation has sought to exert influence throughout Europe and Eurasia, including in the former states of the Soviet Union, by providing resources to political parties, think tanks, and civil society groups that sow distrust in democratic institutions and actors, promote xenophobic and illiberal views, and otherwise undermine European unity. The Government of the Russian Federation has also engaged in well-documented corruption practices as a means toward undermining and buying influence

in European and Eurasian countries.

(2) The Government of the Russian Federation has largely eliminated a once-vibrant Russian-language independent media sector and severely curtails free and independent media within the borders of the Russian Federation. Russian-language media organizations that are funded and controlled by the Government of the Russian Federation and disseminate information within and outside of the Russian Federation routinely traffic in anti-Western disinformation, while few independent, fact-based media sources provide objective reporting for Russian-speaking audiences inside or outside of the Russian Federation.

(3) The Government of the Russian Federation continues to violate its commitments under the Memorandum on Security Assurances in connection with Ukraine's Accession to the Treaty on the Non-Proliferation of Nuclear Weapons, done at Budapest December 5, 1994, and the Conference on Security and Co-operation in Europe Final Act, concluded at Helsinki August 1, 1975 (commonly referred to as the "Helsinki Final Act"), which laid the ground-work for the establishment of the Organization for Security and Co-operation in Europe, of which the Russian Federation is a member, by its illegal annexation of Crimea in 2014, its illegal occupation of South Ossetia and Abkhazia in Georgia in 2008, and its ongoing destabilizing activities in eastern Ukraine.

(4) The Government of the Russian Federation continues to ignore the terms of the August 2008 ceasefire agreement relating to Georgia, which requires the withdrawal of Russian Federation troops, free access by humanitarian groups to the regions of South

Ossetia and Abkhazia, and monitoring of the conflict areas by the European Union Monitoring Mission.

(5) The Government of the Russian Federation is failing to comply with the terms of the Minsk Agreement to address the ongoing conflict in eastern Ukraine, signed in Minsk, Belarus, on February 11, 2015, by the leaders of Ukraine, Russia, France, and Germany, as well as the Minsk Protocol, which was agreed to on September 5, 2014.

(6) The Government of the Russian Federation is—

(A) in violation of the Treaty between the United States of America and the Union of Soviet Socialist Republics on the Elimination of their Intermediate-Range and Shorter-Range Missiles, signed at Washington December 8, 1987, and entered into force June 1, 1988 (commonly known as the "INF Treaty"); and

(B) failing to meet its obligations under the Treaty on Open Skies, done at Helsinki March 24, 1992, and entered into force January 1, 2002 (commonly known as the "Open Skies Treaty").

SEC. 252. SENSE OF CONGRESS.

It is the sense of Congress that—

(1) the Government of the Russian Federation bears responsibility for the continuing violence in Eastern Ukraine, including the death on April 24, 2017, of Joseph Stone, a citizen of the United States working as a monitor for the Organization for Security and Co-

operation in Europe;

(2) the President should call on the Government of the Russian Federation—

(A) to withdraw all of its forces from the territories of Georgia, Ukraine, and Moldova;

(B) to return control of the borders of those territories to their respective governments; and

(C) to cease all efforts to undermine the popularly elected governments of those countries;

(3) the Government of the Russian Federation has applied, and continues to apply, to the countries and peoples of Georgia and Ukraine, traditional uses of force, intelligence operations, and influence campaigns, which represent clear and present threats to the countries of Europe and Eurasia;

(4) in response, the countries of Europe and Eurasia should redouble efforts to build resilience within their institutions, political systems, and civil societies;

(5) the United States supports the institutions that the Government of the Russian Federation seeks to undermine, including the North Atlantic Treaty Organization and the European Union;

(6) a strong North Atlantic Treaty Organization is critical to maintaining peace and security in Europe and Eurasia;

(7) the United States should continue to work with the European Union as a partner against aggression by the

Government of the Russian Federation, coordinating aid programs, development assistance, and other counter-Russian efforts;

(8) the United States should encourage the establishment of a commission for media freedom within the Council of Europe, modeled on the Venice Commission regarding rule of law issues, that would be chartered to provide governments with expert recommendations on maintaining legal and regulatory regimes supportive of free and independent media and an informed citizenry able to distinguish between fact-based reporting, opinion, and disinformation;

(9) in addition to working to strengthen the North Atlantic Treaty Organization and the European Union, the United States should work with the individual countries of Europe and Eurasia—

(A) to identify vulnerabilities to aggression, disinformation, corruption, and so-called hybrid warfare by the Government of the Russian Federation;

(B) to establish strategic and technical plans for addressing those vulnerabilities;

(C) to ensure that the financial systems of those countries are not being used to shield illicit financial activity by officials of the Government of the Russian Federation or individuals in President Vladimir Putin's inner circle who have been enriched through corruption;

(D) to investigate and prosecute cases of corruption by Russian actors; and

(E) to work toward full compliance with the Convention on Combating Bribery of Foreign Public Officials in International Business Transactions (commonly referred to as the "Anti-Bribery Convention") of the Organization for Economic Co-operation and Development; and

(10) the President of the United States should use the authority of the President to impose sanctions under—

(A) the Sergei Magnitsky Rule of Law Accountability Act of 2012 (title IV of Public Law 112–208; 22 U.S.C. 5811 note); and

(B) the Global Magnitsky Human Rights Accountability Act (subtitle F of title XII of Public Law 114–328; 22 U.S.C. 2656 note).

SEC. 253. STATEMENT OF POLICY.

The United States, consistent with the principle of ex injuria jus non oritur, supports the policy known as the "Stimson Doctrine" and thus does not recognize territorial changes effected by force, including the illegal invasions and occupations of Abkhazia, South Ossetia, Crimea, Eastern Ukraine, and Transnistria.

SEC. 254. COORDINATING AID AND ASSISTANCE ACROSS EUROPE AND EURASIA.

(a) AUTHORIZATION OF APPROPRIATIONS.—There are authorized to be appropriated for the Countering Russian Influence Fund $250,000,000 for fiscal years

2018 and 2019.

(b) USE OF FUNDS.—Amounts in the Countering Russian Influence Fund shall be used to effectively implement, prioritized in the following order and subject to the availability of funds, the following goals:

(1) To assist in protecting critical infrastructure and electoral mechanisms from cyberattacks in the following countries:

(A) Countries that are members of the North Atlantic Treaty Organization or the European Union that the Secretary of State determines—

(i) are vulnerable to influence by the Russian Federation; and

(ii) lack the economic capability to effectively respond to aggression by the Russian Federation without the support of the United States.

(B) Countries that are participating in the enlargement process of the North Atlantic Treaty Organization or the European Union, including Albania, Bosnia and Herzegovina, Georgia, Macedonia, Moldova, Kosovo, Serbia, and Ukraine.

(2) To combat corruption, improve the rule of law, and otherwise strengthen independent judiciaries and prosecutors general offices in the countries described in paragraph (1).

(3) To respond to the humanitarian crises and instability caused or aggravated by the invasions and occupations of Georgia and Ukraine by the Russian

Federation.

(4) To improve participatory legislative processes and legal education, political transparency and competition, and compliance with international obligations in the countries described in paragraph (1).

(5) To build the capacity of civil society, media, and other nongovernmental organizations countering the influence and propaganda of the Russian Federation to combat corruption, prioritize access to truthful information, and operate freely in all regions in the countries described in paragraph (1).

(6) To assist the Secretary of State in executing the functions specified in section 1287(b) of the National Defense Authorization Act for Fiscal Year 2017 (Public Law 114–328; 22 U.S.C. 2656 note) for the purposes of recognizing, understanding, exposing, and countering propaganda and disinformation efforts by foreign governments, in coordination with the relevant regional Assistant Secretary or Assistant Secretaries of the Department of State.

(c) REVISION OF ACTIVITIES FOR WHICH AMOUNTS MAY BE USED.—The Secretary of State may modify the goals described in subsection (b) if, not later than 15 days before revising such a goal, the Secretary notifies the appropriate congressional committees of the revision.

(d) IMPLEMENTATION.—

(1) IN GENERAL.—The Secretary of State shall, acting through the Coordinator of United States Assistance to Europe and Eurasia (authorized pursuant

to section 601 of the Support for East European Democracy (SEED) Act of 1989 (22 U.S.C. 5461) and section 102 of the Freedom for Russia and Emerging Eurasian Democracies and Open Markets Support Act of 1992 (22 U.S.C. 5812)), and in consultation with the Administrator for the United States Agency for International Development, the Director of the Global Engagement Center of the Department of State, the Secretary of Defense, the Chairman of the Broadcasting Board of Governors, and the heads of other relevant Federal agencies, coordinate and carry out activities to achieve the goals described in subsection (b).

(2) METHOD.—Activities to achieve the goals described in subsection (b) shall be carried out through—

(A) initiatives of the United States Government;

(B) Federal grant programs such as the Information Access Fund; or

(C) nongovernmental or international organizations, such as the Organization for Security and Co-operation in Europe, the National Endowment for Democracy, the Black Sea Trust, the Balkan Trust for Democracy, the Prague Civil Society Centre, the North Atlantic Treaty Organization Strategic Communications Centre of Excellence, the European Endowment for Democracy, and related organizations.

(3) REPORT ON IMPLEMENTATION.—

(A) IN GENERAL.—Not later than April 1 of each

year, the Secretary of State, acting through the Coordinator of United States Assistance to Europe and Eurasia, shall submit to the appropriate congressional committees a report on the programs and activities carried out to achieve the goals described in subsection (b) during the preceding fiscal year.

(B) ELEMENTS.—Each report required by subparagraph (A) shall include, with respect to each program or activity described in that subparagraph—

(i) the amount of funding for the program or activity;

(ii) the goal described in subsection (b) to which the program or activity relates; and

(iii) an assessment of whether or not the goal was met.

(e) Coordination with global partners.—

(1) IN GENERAL.—In order to maximize cost efficiency, eliminate duplication, and speed the achievement of the goals described in subsection (b), the Secretary of State shall ensure coordination with—

(A) the European Union and its institutions;

(B) the governments of countries that are members of the North Atlantic Treaty Organization or the European Union; and

(C) international organizations and quasi-governmental funding entities that carry out programs and activities that seek to accomplish the goals described in subsection (b).

(2) REPORT BY SECRETARY OF STATE.—Not later than April 1 of each year, the Secretary of State shall submit to the appropriate congressional committees a report that includes—

(A) the amount of funding provided to each country referred to in subsection (b) by—

(i) the European Union or its institutions;

(ii) the government of each country that is a member of the European Union or the North Atlantic Treaty Organization; and

(iii) international organizations and quasi-governmental funding entities that carry out programs and activities that seek to accomplish the goals described in subsection (b); and

(B) an assessment of whether the funding described in subparagraph (A) is commensurate with funding provided by the United States for those goals.

(f) Rule of construction.—Nothing in this section shall be construed to apply to or limit United States foreign assistance not provided using amounts available in the Countering Russian Influence Fund.

(g) Ensuring adequate staffing for governance activities.—In order to ensure that the United States Government is properly focused on combating corruption, improving rule of law, and building the capacity of civil society, media, and other nongovernmental organizations in countries described in subsection (b)(1), the Secretary of State shall establish a pilot program for Foreign Service officer positions focused on governance and anticorruption activities in such countries.

SEC 255. REPORT ON MEDIA ORGANIZATIONS CONTROLLED AND FUNDED BY THE GOVERNMENT OF THE RUSSIAN FEDERATION.

(a) IN GENERAL.—Not later than 90 days after the date of the enactment of this Act, and annually thereafter, the President shall submit to the appropriate congressional committees a report that includes a description of media organizations that are controlled and funded by the Government of the Russian Federation, and any affiliated entities, whether operating within or outside the Russian Federation, including broadcast and satellite-based television, radio, Internet, and print media organizations.

(b) FORM OF REPORT.—The report required by subsection (a) shall be submitted in unclassified form but may include a classified annex.

SEC. 256. REPORT ON RUSSIAN FEDERATION INFLUENCE ON ELECTIONS IN EUROPE AND EURASIA.

(a) IN GENERAL.—Not later than 90 days after the date of the enactment of this Act, and annually thereafter, the President shall submit to the appropriate congressional committees and leadership a report on funds provided by, or funds the use of which was directed by, the Government of the Russian Federation or any Russian person with the intention of influencing the outcome of any election or campaign in any country in Europe or Eurasia during the preceding year, including through direct support to any political party, candidate, lobbying campaign, nongovernmental organization, or civic organization.

(b) FORM OF REPORT.—Each report required by subsection (a) shall be submitted in unclassified form but may include a classified annex.

(c) DEFINITIONS.—In this section:

(1) APPROPRIATE CONGRESSIONAL COMMITTEES AND LEADERSHIP.—The term "appropriate congressional committees and leadership" means—

(A) the Committee on Foreign Relations, the Committee on Banking, Housing, and Urban Affairs, the Committee on Armed Services, the Committee on Homeland Security and Governmental Affairs, the Committee on Appropriations, the Select Committee on Intelligence, and the majority and minority leaders of the Senate; and

(B) the Committee on Foreign Affairs, the Committee on Financial Services, the Committee on Armed Services, the Committee on Homeland Security, the Committee on Appropriations, the Permanent Select Committee on Intelligence, and the Speaker, the majority leader, and the minority leader of the House of Representatives.

(2) RUSSIAN PERSON.—The term "Russian person" means—

(A) an individual who is a citizen or national of the Russian Federation; or

(B) an entity organized under the laws of the Russian Federation or otherwise subject to the jurisdiction of the Government of the Russian Federation.

SEC. 257. UKRANIAN ENERGY SECURITY.

(a) STATEMENT OF POLICY.—It is the policy of the United States—

(1) to support the Government of Ukraine in restoring its sovereign and territorial integrity;

(2) to condemn and oppose all of the destabilizing efforts by the Government of the Russian Federation in Ukraine in violation of its obligations and international commitments;

(3) to never recognize the illegal annexation of Crimea by the Government of the Russian Federation or the separation of any portion of Ukrainian territory through the use of military force;

(4) to deter the Government of the Russian Federation from further destabilizing and invading Ukraine and other independent countries in Central and Eastern Europe and the Caucuses;

(5) to assist in promoting reform in regulatory oversight and operations in Ukraine's energy sector,

including the establishment and empowerment of an independent regulatory organization;

(6) to encourage and support fair competition, market liberalization, and reliability in Ukraine's energy sector;

(7) to help Ukraine and United States allies and partners in Europe reduce their dependence on Russian energy resources, especially natural gas, which the Government of the Russian Federation uses as a weapon to coerce, intimidate, and influence other countries;

(8) to work with European Union member states and European Union institutions to promote energy security through developing diversified and liberalized energy markets that provide diversified sources, suppliers, and routes;

(9) to continue to oppose the NordStream 2 pipeline given its detrimental impacts on the European Union's energy security, gas market development in Central and Eastern Europe, and energy reforms in Ukraine; and

(10) that the United States Government should prioritize the export of United States energy resources in order to create American jobs, help United States allies and partners, and strengthen United States foreign policy.

(b) PLAN TO PROMOTE ENERGY SECURITY IN UKRAINE.—

(1) IN GENERAL.—The Secretary of State, in coordination with the Administrator of the United

States Agency for International Development and the Secretary of Energy, shall work with the Government of Ukraine to develop a plan to increase energy security in Ukraine, increase the amount of energy produced in Ukraine, and reduce Ukraine's reliance on energy imports from the Russian Federation.

(2) ELEMENTS.—The plan developed under paragraph (1) shall include strategies for market liberalization, effective regulation and oversight, supply diversification, energy reliability, and energy efficiency, such as through supporting—

(A) the promotion of advanced technology and modern operating practices in Ukraine's oil and gas sector;

(B) modern geophysical and meteorological survey work as needed followed by international tenders to help attract qualified investment into exploration and development of areas with untapped resources in Ukraine;

(C) a broadening of Ukraine's electric power transmission interconnection with Europe;

(D) the strengthening of Ukraine's capability to maintain electric power grid stability and reliability;

(E) independent regulatory oversight and operations of Ukraine's gas market and electricity sector;

(F) the implementation of primary gas law including pricing, tariff structure, and legal regulatory implementation;

(G) privatization of government owned energy

companies through credible legal frameworks and a transparent process compliant with international best practices;

(H) procurement and transport of emergency fuel supplies, including reverse pipeline flows from Europe;

(I) provision of technical assistance for crisis planning, crisis response, and public outreach;

(J) repair of infrastructure to enable the transport of fuel supplies;

(K) repair of power generating or power transmission equipment or facilities; and

(L) improved building energy efficiency and other measures designed to reduce energy demand in Ukraine.

(3) **REPORTS.—**

(A) IMPLEMENTATION OF UKRAINE FREEDOM SUPPORT ACT OF 2014 PROVISIONS.—Not later than 180 days after the date of the enactment of this Act, the Secretary of State shall submit to the appropriate congressional committees a report detailing the status of implementing the provisions required under section 7(c) of the Ukraine Freedom Support Act of 2014 (22 U.S.C. 8926(c)), including detailing the plans required under that section, the level of funding that has been allocated to and expended for the strategies set forth under that section, and progress that has been made in implementing the strategies developed pursuant to that section.

(B) IN GENERAL.—Not later than 180 days after the date of the enactment of this Act, and every 180 days thereafter, the Secretary of State shall submit to the appropriate congressional committees a report detailing the plan developed under paragraph (1), the level of funding that has been allocated to and expended for the strategies set forth in paragraph (2), and progress that has been made in implementing the strategies.

(C) BRIEFINGS.—The Secretary of State, or a designee of the Secretary, shall brief the appropriate congressional committees not later than 30 days after the submission of each report under subparagraph (B). In addition, the Department of State shall make relevant officials available upon request to brief the appropriate congressional committees on all available information that relates directly or indirectly to Ukraine or energy security in Eastern Europe.

(D) APPROPRIATE CONGRESSIONAL COMMITTEES DEFINED.—In this paragraph, the term "appropriate congressional committees" means—

(i) the Committee on Foreign Relations and the Committee on Appropriations of the Senate; and

(ii) the Committee on Foreign Affairs and the Committee on Appropriations of the House of Representatives.

(c) Supporting efforts of countries in europe and eurasia To decrease their dependence on Russian sources of energy.—

(1) FINDINGS.—Congress makes the following

findings:

(A) The Government of the Russian Federation uses its strong position in the energy sector as leverage to manipulate the internal politics and foreign relations of the countries of Europe and Eurasia.

(B) This influence is based not only on the Russian Federation's oil and natural gas resources, but also on its state-owned nuclear power and electricity companies.

(2) SENSE OF CONGRESS.—It is the sense of Congress that—

(A) the United States should assist the efforts of the countries of Europe and Eurasia to enhance their energy security through diversification of energy supplies in order to lessen dependencies on Russian Federation energy resources and state-owned entities; and

(B) the Export-Import Bank of the United States and the Overseas Private Investment Corporation should play key roles in supporting critical energy projects that contribute to that goal.

(3) USE OF COUNTERING RUSSIAN INFLUENCE FUND TO PROVIDE TECHNICAL ASSISTANCE.— Amounts in the Countering Russian Influence Fund pursuant to section 254 shall be used to provide technical advice to countries described in subsection (b)(1) of such section designed to enhance energy security and lessen dependence on energy from Russian Federation sources.

(d) Authorization of appropriations.—There is authorized to be appropriated for the Department of State a total of $30,000,000 for fiscal years 2018 and 2019 to carry out the strategies set forth in subsection (b)(2) and other activities under this section related to the promotion of energy security in Ukraine.

(e) Rule of construction.—Nothing in this section shall be construed as affecting the responsibilities required and authorities provided under section 7 of the Ukraine Freedom Support Act of 2014 (22 U.S.C. 8926).

SEC. 258. TERMINATION.

The provisions of this subtitle shall terminate on the date that is 5 years after the date of the enactment of this Act.

SEC. 259. APPROPRIATE CONGRESSIONAL COMMITTEES DEFINED.

Except as otherwise provided, in this subtitle, the term "appropriate congressional committees" means—

(1) the Committee on Foreign Relations, the Committee on Banking, Housing, and Urban Affairs, the Committee on Armed Services, the Committee on Homeland Security and Governmental Affairs, the Committee on Appropriations, and the Select Committee on Intelligence of the Senate; and

(2) the Committee on Foreign Affairs, the Committee on Financial Services, the Committee on Armed Services, the Committee on Homeland Security, the

Committee on Appropriations, and the Permanent Select Committee on Intelligence of the House of Representatives.

SUBTITLE C—COMBATING TERRORISM AND ILLICIT FINANCING

PART 1—NATIONAL STRATEGY FOR COMBATING TERRORIST AND OTHER ILLICIT FINANCING

SEC. 261. **DEVELOPMENT OF NATIONAL STRATEGY.**

(a) IN GENERAL.—The President, acting through the Secretary, shall, in consultation with the Attorney General, the Secretary of State, the Secretary of Homeland Security, the Director of National Intelligence, the Director of the Office of Management and Budget, and the appropriate Federal banking agencies and Federal functional regulators, develop a national strategy for combating the financing of terrorism and related forms of illicit finance.

(b) TRANSMITTAL TO CONGRESS.—

(1) IN GENERAL.—Not later than 1 year after the date of the enactment of this Act, the President shall submit to the appropriate congressional committees a comprehensive national strategy developed in accordance with subsection (a).

(2) UPDATES.—Not later than January 31, 2020, and January 31, 2022, the President shall submit to the appropriate congressional committees' updated

versions of the national strategy submitted under paragraph (1).

(c) SEPARATE PRESENTATION OF CLASSIFIED MATERIAL.—Any part of the national strategy that involves information that is properly classified under criteria established by the President shall be submitted to Congress separately in a classified annex and, if requested by the chairman or ranking member of one of the appropriate congressional committees, as a briefing at an appropriate level of security.

SEC. 262. CONTENTS OF NATIONAL STRATEGY.

The strategy described in section 261 shall contain the following:

(1) EVALUATION OF EXISTING EFFORTS.—An assessment of the effectiveness of and ways in which the United States is currently addressing the highest levels of risk of various forms of illicit finance, including those identified in the documents entitled "2015 National Money Laundering Risk Assessment" and "2015 National Terrorist Financing Risk Assessment", published by the Department of the Treasury and a description of how the strategy is integrated into, and supports, the broader counter terrorism strategy of the United States.

(2) GOALS, OBJECTIVES, AND PRIORITIES.—A comprehensive, research-based, long-range, quantifiable discussion of goals, objectives, and

priorities for disrupting and preventing illicit finance activities within and transiting the financial system of the United States that outlines priorities to reduce the incidence, dollar value, and effects of illicit finance.

(3) THREATS.—An identification of the most significant illicit finance threats to the financial system of the United States.

(4) REVIEWS AND PROPOSED CHANGES.— Reviews of enforcement efforts, relevant regulations and relevant provisions of law and, if appropriate, discussions of proposed changes determined to be appropriate to ensure that the United States pursues coordinated and effective efforts at all levels of government, and with international partners of the United States, in the fight against illicit finance.

(5) DETECTION AND PROSECUTION INITIATIVES.—A description of efforts to improve, as necessary, detection and prosecution of illicit finance, including efforts to ensure that—

(A) subject to legal restrictions, all appropriate data collected by the Federal Government that is relevant to the efforts described in this section be available in a timely fashion to—

(i) all appropriate Federal departments and agencies; and

(ii) as appropriate and consistent with section 314 of the International Money Laundering Abatement and Financial Anti-Terrorism Act of 2001 (31 U.S.C. 5311 note), to financial institutions to assist the financial institutions in efforts to comply with laws aimed at curbing illicit finance; and

(B) appropriate efforts are undertaken to ensure that Federal departments and agencies charged with reducing and preventing illicit finance make thorough use of publicly available data in furtherance of this effort.

(6) THE ROLE OF THE PRIVATE FINANCIAL SECTOR IN PREVENTION OF ILLICIT FINANCE.—A discussion of ways to enhance partnerships between the private financial sector and Federal departments and agencies with regard to the prevention and detection of illicit finance, including—

(A) efforts to facilitate compliance with laws aimed at stopping such illicit finance while maintaining the effectiveness of such efforts; and

(B) providing guidance to strengthen internal controls and to adopt on an industry-wide basis more effective policies.

(7) ENHANCEMENT OF INTERGOVERNMENTAL COOPERATION.—A discussion of ways to combat illicit finance by enhancing—

(A) cooperative efforts between and among Federal, State, and local officials, including State regulators, State and local prosecutors, and other law enforcement officials; and

(B) cooperative efforts with and between governments of countries and with and between multinational institutions with expertise in fighting illicit finance, including the Financial Action Task Force and the Egmont Group of Financial Intelligence Units.

(8) TREND ANALYSIS OF EMERGING ILLICIT FINANCE THREATS.—A discussion of and data regarding trends in illicit finance, including evolving forms of value transfer such as so-called cryptocurrencies, other methods that are computer, telecommunications, or Internet-based, cyber crime, or any other threats that the Secretary may choose to identify.

(9) BUDGET PRIORITIES.—A multiyear budget plan that identifies sufficient resources needed to successfully execute the full range of missions called for in this section.

(10) TECHNOLOGY ENHANCEMENTS.—An analysis of current and developing ways to leverage technology to improve the effectiveness of efforts to stop the financing of terrorism and other forms of illicit finance, including better integration of open-source data.

PART 2—ENHANCING ANTITERRORISM TOOLS OF THE DEPARTMENT OF THE TREASURY

SEC. 271. IMPROVING ANTITERROR FINANCE MONITORING OF FUNDS TRANSFERS.

(a) STUDY.—

(1) IN GENERAL.—To improve the ability of the

Department of the Treasury to better track cross-border fund transfers and identify potential financing of terrorist or other forms of illicit finance, the Secretary shall carry out a study to assess—

(A) the potential efficacy of requiring banking regulators to establish a pilot program to provide technical assistance to depository institutions and credit unions that wish to provide account services to money services businesses serving individuals in Somalia;

(B) whether such a pilot program could be a model for improving the ability of United States persons to make legitimate funds transfers through transparent and easily monitored channels while preserving strict compliance with the Bank Secrecy Act (Public Law 91–508; 84 Stat. 1114) and related controls aimed at stopping money laundering and the financing of terrorism; and

(C) consistent with current legal requirements regarding confidential supervisory information, the potential impact of allowing money services businesses to share certain State examination information with depository institutions and credit unions, or whether another appropriate mechanism could be identified to allow a similar exchange of information to give the depository institutions and credit unions a better understanding of whether an individual money services business is adequately meeting its anti-money laundering and counter-terror financing obligations to combat money laundering, the financing of terror, or related illicit finance.

(2) PUBLIC INPUT.—The Secretary should solicit and consider public input as appropriate in developing the

study required under subsection (a).

(b) Report.—Not later than 270 days after the date of the enactment of this Act, the Secretary shall submit to the Committee on Banking, Housing, and Urban Affairs and the Committee on Foreign Relations of the Senate and the Committee on Financial Services and the Committee on Foreign Affairs of the House of Representatives a report that contains all findings and determinations made in carrying out the study required under subsection (a).

SEC. 272. SENSE OF CONGRESS ON INTERNATIONAL COOPERATION REGARDING TERRORIST FINANCING INTELLIGENCE.

It is the sense of Congress that the Secretary, acting through the Under Secretary for Terrorism and Financial Crimes, should intensify work with foreign partners to help the foreign partners develop intelligence analytic capacities, in a financial intelligence unit, finance ministry, or other appropriate agency, that are—

(1) commensurate to the threats faced by the foreign partner; and

(2) designed to better integrate intelligence efforts with the anti-money laundering and counter-terrorist financing regimes of the foreign partner.

SEC.273. EXAMINING THE COUNTER-TERROR FINANCING ROLE OF THE DEPARTMENT OF THE TREASURY IN EMBASSIES.

Not later than 180 days after the date of the enactment of this Act, the Secretary shall submit to the Committee on Banking, Housing, and Urban Affairs and the Committee on Foreign Relations of the Senate and the Committee on Financial Services and the Committee on Foreign Affairs of the House of Representatives a report that contains—

(1) a list of the United States embassies in which a full-time Department of the Treasury financial attaché is stationed and a description of how the interests of the Department of the Treasury relating to terrorist financing and money laundering are addressed (via regional attachés or otherwise) at United States embassies where no such attachés are present;

(2) a list of the United States embassies at which the Department of the Treasury has assigned a technical assistance advisor from the Office of Technical Assistance of the Department of the Treasury;

(3) an overview of how Department of the Treasury financial attachés and technical assistance advisors assist in efforts to counter illicit finance, to include money laundering, terrorist financing, and proliferation financing; and

(4) an overview of patterns, trends, or other issues identified by the Department of the Treasury and whether resources are sufficient to address these issues.

SEC. 274. INCLUSION OF SECRETARY OF THE TREASURY ON THE NATIONAL SECURITY COUNCIL.

(a) IN GENERAL.—Section 101(c)(1) of the National Security Act of 1947 (50 U.S.C. 3021(c)(1)) is amended by inserting "the Secretary of the Treasury," before "and such other officers".

(b) RULE OF CONSTRUCTION.—The amendment made by subsection (a) may not be construed to authorize the National Security Council to have a professional staff level that exceeds the limitation set forth under section 101(e)(3) of the National Security Act of 1947 (50 U.S.C. 3021(e)(3)).

SEC. 275. INCLUSION OF ALL FUNDS.

(a) IN GENERAL.—Section 5326 of title 31, United States Code, is amended—

(1) in the heading of such section, by striking "coin and currency";

(2) in subsection (a)—

(A) by striking "subtitle and" and inserting "subtitle or to"; and

(B) in paragraph (1)(A), by striking "United States coins or currency (or such other monetary instruments as the Secretary may describe in such order)" and inserting "funds (as the Secretary may describe in such order),"; and

(3) in subsection (b)—

(A) in paragraph (1)(A), by striking "coins or currency (or monetary instruments)" and inserting "funds"; and

(B) in paragraph (2), by striking "coins or currency (or such other monetary instruments as the Secretary may describe in the regulation or order)" and inserting "funds (as the Secretary may describe in the regulation or order)".

(b) CLERICAL AMENDMENT.—The table of contents for chapter 53 of title 31, United States Code, is amended in the item relating to section 5326 by striking "coin and currency".

PART 3—DEFINITIONS

SEC. 281. DEFINITIONS.

In this subtitle—

(1) THE TERM "APPROPRIATE CONGRESSIONAL COMMITTEES" MEANS—

(A) the Committee on Banking, Housing, and Urban Affairs, the Committee on Foreign Relations, Committee on Armed Services, Committee on the Judiciary, Committee on Homeland Security and Governmental Affairs, and the Select Committee on Intelligence of the Senate; and

(B) the Committee on Financial Services, the Committee on Foreign Affairs, the Committee on Armed Services, the Committee on the Judiciary, Committee on Homeland Security, and the Permanent Select Committee on Intelligence of the House of Representatives;

(2) the term "appropriate Federal banking agencies" has the meaning given the term in section 3 of the Federal Deposit Insurance Act (12 U.S.C. 1813);

(3) the term "Bank Secrecy Act" means—

(A) section 21 of the Federal Deposit Insurance Act (12 U.S.C. 1829b);

(B) chapter 2 of title I of Public Law 91–508 (12 U.S.C. 1951 et seq.); and

(C) subchapter II of chapter 53 of title 31, United States Code;

(4) the term "Federal functional regulator" has the meaning given that term in section 509 of the Gramm-Leach-Bliley Act (15 U.S.C. 6809);

(5) the term "illicit finance" means the financing of terrorism, narcotics trafficking, or proliferation, money laundering, or other forms of illicit financing domestically or internationally, as defined by the President;

(6) the term "money services business" has the meaning given the term under section 1010.100 of title 31, Code of Federal Regulations;

(7) the term "Secretary" means the Secretary of the Treasury; and

(8) the term "State" means each of the several States, the District of Columbia, and each territory or possession of the United States.

SUBTITLE D—RULE OF CONSTRUCTION

SEC. **291. RULE OF CONSTRUCTION.**

Nothing in this title or the amendments made by this title (other than sections 216 and 236(b)) shall be construed to limit the authority of the President under the International Emergency Economic Powers Act (50 U.S.C. 1701 et seq.).

SEC. 292. Sense of Congress on the strategic importance of Article 5 of the North Atlantic Treaty.

(a) Findings.—Congress makes the following findings:

(1) The principle of collective defense of the North Atlantic Treaty Organization (NATO) is immortalized in Article 5 of the North Atlantic Treaty in which members pledge that "an armed attack against one or more of them in Europe or North America shall be considered an attack against them all".

(2) For almost 7 decades, the principle of collective defense has effectively served as a strategic deterrent for the member nations of the North Atlantic Treaty

Organization and provided stability throughout the world, strengthening the security of the United States and all 28 other member nations.

(3) Following the September 11, 2001, terrorist attacks in New York, Washington, and Pennsylvania, the Alliance agreed to invoke Article 5 for the first time, affirming its commitment to collective defense.

(4) Countries that are members of the North Atlantic Treaty Organization have made historic contributions and sacrifices while combating terrorism in Afghanistan through the International Security Assistance Force and the Resolute Support Mission.

(5) The recent attacks in the United Kingdom underscore the importance of an international alliance to combat hostile nation states and terrorist groups.

(6) At the 2014 NATO summit in Wales, the member countries of the North Atlantic Treaty Organization decided that all countries that are members of NATO would spend an amount equal to 2 percent of their gross domestic product on defense by 2024.

(7) Collective defense unites the 29 members of the North Atlantic Treaty Organization, each committing to protecting and supporting one another from external adversaries, which bolsters the North Atlantic Alliance.

(b) Sense of Congress.—It is the sense of Congress—

(1) to express the vital importance of Article 5 of the North Atlantic Treaty, the charter of the North Atlantic Treaty Organization, as it continues to serve as a critical deterrent to potential hostile nations and

terrorist organizations;

(2) to remember the first and only invocation of Article 5 by the North Atlantic Treaty Organization in support of the United States after the terrorist attacks of September 11, 2001;

(3) to affirm that the United States remains fully committed to the North Atlantic Treaty Organization and will honor its obligations enshrined in Article 5; and

(4) to condemn any threat to the sovereignty, territorial integrity, freedom, or democracy of any country that is a member of the North Atlantic Treaty Organization.

TITLE III—SANCTIONS WITH RESPECT TO NORTH KOREA

SEC. 301. **SHORT TITLE**.

This title may be cited as the "Korean Interdiction and Modernization of Sanctions Act".

SEC. 302. **DEFINITIONS**.

(a) Amendments to definitions in the North Korea Sanctions and Policy Enhancement Act of 2016.—

(1) APPLICABLE EXECUTIVE ORDER.—Section 3(1)(A) of the North Korea Sanctions and Policy Enhancement Act of 2016 (22 U.S.C. 9202(1)(A)) is amended—

(A) by striking "or Executive Order 13694" and inserting "Executive Order No. 13694"; and

(B) by inserting "or Executive Order No. 13722 (50 U.S.C. 1701 note; relating to blocking the property of the Government of North Korea and the Workers' Party of Korea, and Prohibiting Certain Transactions With Respect to North Korea)," before "to the extent".

(2) APPLICABLE UNITED NATIONS SECURITY COUNCIL RESOLUTION.—Section 3(2)(A) of the North Korea Sanctions and Policy Enhancement Act of 2016 (22 U.S.C. 9202(2)(A)) is amended by striking "or 2094 (2013)" and inserting "2094 (2013), 2270 (2016), or 2321 (2016)".

(3) FOREIGN PERSON.—Section 3 of the North Korea Sanctions and Policy Enhancement Act of 2016 (22 U.S.C. 9202) is amended—

(A) by redesignating paragraphs (5) through (14) as paragraphs (6) through (15), respectively; and

(B) by inserting after paragraph (4) the following new paragraph:

"(5) FOREIGN PERSON.—The term 'foreign person' means—

"(A) an individual who is not a United States citizen or an alien lawfully admitted for permanent residence to the United States; or

"(B) an entity that is not a United States person.".

(4) LUXURY GOODS.—Paragraph (9) of section 3 of the North Korea Sanctions and Policy Enhancement Act of 2016 (22 U.S.C. 9202), as redesignated by paragraph (3) of this subsection, is amended—

(A) in subparagraph (A), by striking "and" at the end;

(B) in subparagraph (B), by striking the period at the end and inserting "; and"; and

(C) by adding at the end the following new subparagraph:

"(C) also includes any items so designated under an applicable United Nations Security Council resolution.".

(5) NORTH KOREAN PERSON.—Section 3 of the North Korea Sanctions and Policy Enhancement Act of 2016 (22 U.S.C. 9202), as amended by paragraph (3) of this subsection, is further amended—

(A) by redesignating paragraphs (13) through (15) as paragraphs (14) through (16), respectively; and

(B) by inserting after paragraph (12) the following new paragraph:

"(13) NORTH KOREAN PERSON.—The term 'North Korean person' means—

"(A) a North Korean citizen or national; or

"(B) an entity owned or controlled by the Government of North Korea or by a North Korean citizen or national.".

(b) Definitions for purposes of this Act.—In this title:

(1) APPLICABLE UNITED NATIONS SECURITY COUNCIL RESOLUTION; LUXURY GOODS.—The terms "applicable United Nations Security Council resolution" and "luxury goods" have the meanings given those terms, respectively, in section 3 of the North Korea Sanctions and Policy Enhancement Act of 2016 (22 U.S.C. 9202), as amended by subsection (a).

(2) APPROPRIATE CONGRESSIONAL COMMITTEES; GOVERNMENT OF NORTH KOREA; UNITED STATES PERSON.—The terms "appropriate congressional committees", "Government of North Korea", and "United States person" have the

meanings given those terms, respectively, in section 3 of the North Korea Sanctions and Policy Enhancement Act of 2016 (22 U.S.C. 9202).

(3) FOREIGN PERSON; NORTH KOREAN PERSON.—The terms "foreign person" and "North Korean person" have the meanings given those terms, respectively, in paragraph (5) and paragraph (13) of section 3 of the North Korea Sanctions and Policy Enhancement Act of 2016 (22 U.S.C. 9202(5) and 9202(13)), as added by subsection (a).

(4) PROHIBITED WEAPONS PROGRAM.—The term "prohibited weapons program" means—

(A) any program related to the development of nuclear, chemical, or biological weapons, and their means of delivery, including ballistic missiles; and

(B) any program to develop related materials with respect to a program described in subparagraph (A).

subtitle A—Sanctions to enforce and implement United Nations Security Council sanctions against North Korea

SEC. 311. MODIFICATION AND EXPANSION OF REQUIREMENTS FOR THE DESIGNATION OF PERSONS.

(a) EXPANSION OF MANDATORY DESIGNATIONS.— Section 104(a) of the North Korea Sanctions and Policy Enhancement Act of 2016 (22 U.S.C. 9214(a)) is amended—

(1) in paragraph (9), by striking "; or" and inserting "or any defense article or defense service (as such terms are defined in section 47 of the Arms Export Control Act (22 U.S.C. 2794));";

(2) by redesignating paragraph (10) as paragraph (15);

(3) by inserting after paragraph (9) the following new paragraphs:

"(10) knowingly, directly or indirectly, purchases or otherwise acquires from North Korea any significant amounts of gold, titanium ore, vanadium ore, copper, silver, nickel, zinc, or rare earth minerals;

"(11) knowingly, directly or indirectly, sells or transfers to North Korea any significant amounts of rocket, aviation, or jet fuel (except for use by a civilian passenger aircraft outside North Korea, exclusively for consumption during its flight to North Korea or its return flight);

"(12) knowingly, directly or indirectly, provides significant amounts of fuel or supplies, provides bunkering services, or facilitates a significant transaction or transactions to operate or maintain, a vessel or aircraft that is designated under an applicable Executive order or an applicable United Nations Security Council resolution, or that is owned or controlled by a person designated under an applicable Executive order or applicable United Nations Security Council resolution;

"(13) knowingly, directly or indirectly, insures, registers, facilitates the registration of, or maintains insurance or a registration for, a vessel owned or controlled by the Government of North Korea, except as specifically approved by the United Nations Security Council;

"(14) knowingly, directly or indirectly, maintains a correspondent account (as defined in section 201A(d)(1)) with any North Korean financial institution, except as specifically approved by the United Nations Security Council; or"; and

(4) in paragraph (15), as so redesignated, by striking "(9)" and inserting "(14)".

(b) EXPANSION OF ADDITIONAL DISCRETIONARY DESIGNATIONS.—

(1) IN GENERAL.—Section 104(b)(1) of the North Korea Sanctions and Policy Enhancement Act of 2016 (22 U.S.C. 9214(b)(1)) is amended—

(A) in subparagraph (A), by striking "pursuant to an applicable United Nations Security Council resolution;" and inserting the following: "pursuant to—

"(i) an applicable United Nations Security Council resolution;

"(ii) any regulation promulgated under section 404; or

"(iii) any applicable Executive order;";

(B) in subparagraph (B)(iii), by striking "or" at the end;

(C) in subparagraph (C), by striking the period at the

end and inserting a semicolon; and

(D) by adding at the end the following new subparagraphs:

"(D) knowingly, directly or indirectly, purchased or otherwise acquired from the Government of North Korea significant quantities of coal, iron, or iron ore, in excess of the limitations provided in applicable United Nations Security Council resolutions;

"(E) knowingly, directly or indirectly, purchased or otherwise acquired significant types or amounts of textiles from the Government of North Korea;

"(F) knowingly facilitated a significant transfer of funds or property of the Government of North Korea that materially contributes to any violation of an applicable United National Security Council resolution;

"(G) knowingly, directly or indirectly, facilitated a significant transfer to or from the Government of North Korea of bulk cash, precious metals, gemstones, or other stores of value not described under subsection (a)(10);

"(H) knowingly, directly or indirectly, sold, transferred, or otherwise provided significant amounts of crude oil, condensates, refined petroleum, other types of petroleum or petroleum byproducts, liquified natural gas, or other natural gas resources to the Government of North Korea (except for heavy fuel oil, gasoline, or diesel fuel for humanitarian use or as excepted under subsection (a)(11));

"(I) knowingly, directly or indirectly, engaged in,

facilitated, or was responsible for the online commercial activities of the Government of North Korea, including online gambling;

"(J) knowingly, directly or indirectly, purchased or otherwise acquired fishing rights from the Government of North Korea;

"(K) knowingly, directly or indirectly, purchased or otherwise acquired significant types or amounts of food or agricultural products from the Government of North Korea;

"(L) knowingly, directly or indirectly, engaged in, facilitated, or was responsible for the exportation of workers from North Korea in a manner intended to generate significant revenue, directly or indirectly, for use by the Government of North Korea or by the Workers' Party of Korea;

"(M) knowingly conducted a significant transaction or transactions in North Korea's transportation, mining, energy, or financial services industries; or

"(N) except as specifically approved by the United Nations Security Council, and other than through a correspondent account as described in subsection (a)(14), knowingly facilitated the operation of any branch, subsidiary, or office of a North Korean financial institution.".

(2) EFFECTIVE DATE.—The amendments made by paragraph (1) take effect on the date of the enactment of this Act and apply with respect to conduct described in subparagraphs (D) through (N) of section 104(b)(1) of the North Korea Sanctions and Policy Enhancement

Act of 2016, as added by paragraph (1), engaged in on or after such date of enactment.

(c) MANDATORY AND DISCRETIONARY ASSET BLOCKING.—Section 104(c) of the North Korea Sanctions and Policy Enhancement Act of 2016 (22 U.S.C. 9214(c)) is amended—

(1) by striking "of a designated person" and inserting "of a person designated under subsection (a)";

(2) by striking "The President" and inserting the following:

"(1) MANDATORY ASSET BLOCKING.—The President"; and

(3) by adding at the end the following new paragraph:

"(2) DISCRETIONARY ASSET BLOCKING.—The President may also exercise such powers, in the same manner and to the same extent described in paragraph (1), with respect to a person designated under subsection (b).".

(d) DESIGNATION OF ADDITIONAL PERSONS.—

(1) IN GENERAL.—Not later than 180 days after the date of the enactment of this Act, the President shall submit to the appropriate congressional committees a report including a determination as to whether reasonable grounds exist, and an explanation of the reasons for any determination that such grounds do not exist, to designate, pursuant to section 104 of the North Korea Sanctions and Policy Enhancement Act of 2016

([22 U.S.C. 9214](#)), as amended by this section, each of the following:

(A) The Korea Shipowners' Protection and Indemnity Association, a North Korean insurance company, with respect to facilitating imports, exports, and reexports of arms and related materiel to and from North Korea, or for other activities prohibited by such section 104.

(B) Chinpo Shipping Company (Private) Limited, a Singapore corporation, with respect to facilitating imports, exports, and reexports of arms and related materiel to and from North Korea.

(C) The Central Bank of the Democratic People's Republic of Korea, with respect to the sale of gold to, the receipt of gold from, or the import or export of gold by the Government of North Korea.

(D) Kumgang Economic Development Corporation (KKG), with respect to being an entity controlled by Bureau 39 of the Workers' Party of the Government of North Korea.

(E) Sam Pa, also known as Xu Jinghua, Xu Songhua, Sa Muxu, Samo, Sampa, or Sam King, and any entities owned or controlled by such individual, with respect to transactions with KKG.

(F) The Chamber of Commerce of the Democratic People's Republic of Korea, with respect to the exportation of workers in violation of section 104(a)(5) or of section 104(b)(1)(M) of such Act, as amended by [subsection (b)](#) of this section.

(2) FORM.—The report submitted under [paragraph (1)](#)

may contain a classified annex.

SEC. 312. PROHIBITION ON INDIRECT CORRESPONDENT ACCOUNTS.

(a) IN GENERAL.—Title II of the North Korea Sanctions and Policy Enhancement Act of 2016 (22 U.S.C. 9221 et seq.) is amended by inserting after section 201 the following new section:

(b)

"SEC. 201A. PROHIBITION ON INDIRECT CORRESPONDENT ACCOUNTS.

"(a) IN GENERAL.—Except as provided in subsection (b), if a United States financial institution has or obtains knowledge that a correspondent account established, maintained, administered, or managed by that institution for a foreign financial institution is being used by the foreign financial institution to provide significant financial services indirectly to any person, foreign government, or financial institution designated under section 104, the United States financial institution shall ensure that such correspondent account is no longer used to provide such services.

"(b) EXCEPTION.—A United States financial institution is authorized to process transfers of funds to or from North Korea, or for the direct or indirect benefit of any person, foreign government, or financial institution that is designated under section 104, only if the transfer—

"(1) arises from, and is ordinarily incident and necessary to give effect to, an underlying transaction that has been authorized by a specific or general license issued by the Secretary of the Treasury; and

"(2) does not involve debiting or crediting a North Korean account.

"(c) DEFINITIONS.—In this section:

"(1) CORRESPONDENT ACCOUNT.—The term 'correspondent account' has the meaning given that term in section 5318A of title 31, United States Code.

"(2) UNITED STATES FINANCIAL INSTITUTION.—The term 'United States financial institution' means has the meaning given that term in section 510.310 of title 31, Code of Federal Regulations, as in effect on the date of the enactment of this section.

"(3) FOREIGN FINANCIAL INSTITUTION.—The term 'foreign financial institution' has the meaning given that term in section 1010.605 of title 31, Code of Federal Regulations, as in effect on the date of the enactment of this section.".

(b) Clerical amendment.—The table of contents in section 1(b) of the North Korea Sanctions and Policy Enhancement Act of 2016 is amended by inserting after the item relating to section 201 the following new item:

"Sec. 201A. Prohibition on indirect correspondent accounts.".

SEC. 313. Limitations on foreign assistance to noncompliant governments.

Section 203 of the North Korea Sanctions and Policy Enhancement Act of 2016 (22 U.S.C. 9223) is amended—

(1) in subsection (b)—

(A) in the heading, by striking "Transactions in Lethal Military Equipment" and inserting "Transactions in Defense Articles or Defense Services";

(B) in paragraph (1), by striking "that provides lethal military equipment to the Government of North Korea" and inserting "that provides to or receives from the Government of North Korea a defense article or defense service, as such terms are defined in section 47 of the Arms Export Control Act (22 U.S.C. 2794), if the President determines that a significant type or amount of such article or service has been so provided or received"; and

(C) in paragraph (2), by striking "1 year" and inserting "2 years";

(2) in subsection (d), by striking "or emergency" and inserting "maternal and child health, disease prevention and response, or"; and

(3) by adding at the end the following new subsection:

"(e) REPORT ON ARMS TRAFFICKING INVOLVING NORTH KOREA.—

"(1) IN GENERAL.—Not later than 180 days after the date of the enactment of this subsection, and annually thereafter for 5 years, the Secretary of State shall submit to the appropriate congressional committees a report that specifically describes the compliance of foreign countries and other foreign jurisdictions with the requirement to curtail the trade described in subsection (b)(1).

"(2) FORM.—The report required under paragraph (1) shall be submitted in unclassified form but may contain a classified annex.".

SEC. 314. AMENDMENTS TO ENHANCE INSPECTION AUTHORITIES.

Title II of the North Korea Sanctions and Policy Enhancement Act of 2016 (22 U.S.C. 9221 et seq.), as amended by section 102 of this Act, is further amended by striking section 205 and inserting the following:

205. ENHANCED INSPECTION AUTHORITIES.

"(a) REPORT REQUIRED.—

"(1) IN GENERAL.—Not later than 180 days after the date of the enactment of this section, and annually thereafter for 5 years, the President shall submit to the appropriate congressional committees a report—

"(A) identifying the operators of foreign sea ports and airports that knowingly—

"(i) significantly fail to implement or enforce

regulations to inspect ships, aircraft, cargo, or conveyances in transit to or from North Korea, as required by applicable United Nations Security Council resolutions;

"(ii) facilitate the transfer, transshipment, or conveyance of significant types or quantities of cargo, vessels, or aircraft owned or controlled by persons designated under applicable United Nations Security Council resolutions; or

"(iii) facilitate any of the activities described in section 104(a);

"(B) describing the extent to which the requirements of applicable United Nations Security Council resolutions to de-register any vessel owned, controlled, or operated by or on behalf of the Government of North Korea have been implemented by other foreign countries;

"(C) describing the compliance of the Islamic Republic of Iran with the sanctions mandated in applicable United Nations Security Council resolutions;

"(D) identifying vessels, aircraft, and conveyances owned or controlled by the Reconnaissance General Bureau of the Workers' Party of Korea; and

"(E) describing the diplomatic and enforcement efforts by the President to secure the full implementation of the applicable United Nations Security Council resolutions, as described in subparagraphs (A) through (C).

"(2) FORM.—The report required under paragraph (1) shall be submitted in unclassified form but may contain a classified annex.

"(b) SPECIFIC FINDINGS.—Each report required under subsection (a) shall include specific findings with respect to the following ports and airports:

"(1) The ports of Dandong, Dalian, and any other port in the People's Republic of China that the President deems appropriate.

"(2) The ports of Abadan, Bandar-e-Abbas, Chabahar, Bandar-e-Khomeini, Bushehr Port, Asaluyeh Port, Kish, Kharg Island, Bandar-e-Lenge, and Khorramshahr, and Tehran Imam Khomeini International Airport, in the Islamic Republic of Iran.

"(3) The ports of Nakhodka, Vanino, and Vladivostok, in the Russian Federation.

"(4) The ports of Latakia, Banias, and Tartous, and Damascus International Airport, in the Syrian Arab Republic.

"(c) ENHANCED SECURITY TARGETING REQUIREMENTS.—

"(1) IN GENERAL.—Except as provided in paragraph (2), the Secretary of Homeland Security may, using a layered approach, require enhanced screening procedures to determine whether physical inspections are warranted of any cargo bound for or landed in the United States that—

"(A) has been transported through a sea port or airport the operator of which has been identified by the President in accordance with subsection (a)(1) as having repeatedly failed to comply with applicable United Nations Security Council resolutions;

"(B) is aboard a vessel or aircraft, or within a conveyance that has, within the last 365 days, entered the territory or waters of North Korea, or landed in any of the sea ports or airports of North Korea; or

"(C) is registered by a country or jurisdiction whose compliance has been identified by the President as deficient pursuant to subsection (a)(2).

"(2) EXCEPTION FOR FOOD, MEDICINE, AND HUMANITARIAN SHIPMENTS.—Paragraph (1) shall not apply to any vessel, aircraft, or conveyance that has entered the territory or waters of North Korea, or landed in any of the sea ports or airports of North Korea, exclusively for the purposes described in section 208(b)(3)(B), or to import food, medicine, or supplies into North Korea to meet the humanitarian needs of the North Korean people.

"(d) SEIZURE AND FORFEITURE.—A vessel, aircraft, or conveyance used to facilitate any of the activities described in section 104(a) under the jurisdiction of the United States may be seized and forfeited, or subject to forfeiture, under—

"(1) chapter 46 of title 18, United States Code; or

"(2) part V of title IV of the Tariff Act of 1930 (19 U.S.C. 1581 et seq.).".

SEC. 315. ENFORCING COMPLIANCE WITH UNITED NATIONS SHIPPING SANCTIONS AGAINST NORTH KOREA.

(a) IN GENERAL.—The Ports and Waterways Safety Act (33 U.S.C. 1221 et seq.) is amended by adding at the end the following new section:

(b)

"SEC. 16. **PROHIBITION ON ENTRY AND OPERATION.**

"(a) PROHIBITION.—

"(1) IN GENERAL.—Except as otherwise provided in this section, no vessel described in subsection (b) may enter or operate in the navigable waters of the United States or transfer cargo in any port or place under the jurisdiction of the United States.

"(2) LIMITATIONS ON APPLICATION.—

"(A) IN GENERAL.—The prohibition under paragraph (1) shall not apply with respect to—

"(i) a vessel described in subsection (b)(1), if the Secretary of State determines that—

"(I) the vessel is owned or operated by or on behalf of a country the government of which the Secretary of State determines is closely cooperating with the United States with respect to implementing the applicable United Nations Security Council resolutions (as such term is defined in section 3 of the North Korea Sanctions and Policy Enhancement Act of 2016); or

"(II) it is in the national security interest not to apply the prohibition to such vessel; or "(ii) a vessel described in subsection (b)(2), if the Secretary of State determines that the vessel is no longer registered as described in that subsection.

"(B) NOTICE.—Not later than 15 days after making a determination under subparagraph (A), the Secretary of State shall submit to the Committee on Foreign Affairs and the Committee on Transportation and Infrastructure of the House of Representatives and the Committee on Foreign Relations and the Committee on Commerce, Science, and Transportation of the Senate written notice of the determination and the basis upon which the determination was made.

"(C) PUBLICATION.—The Secretary of State shall publish a notice in the Federal Register of each determination made under subparagraph (A).

"(b) Vessels described.—A vessel referred to in subsection (a) is a foreign vessel for which a notice of arrival is required to be filed under section 4(a)(5), and that—

"(1) is on the most recent list of vessels published in Federal Register under subsection (c)(2); or

"(2) more than 180 days after the publication of such list, is knowingly registered, pursuant to the 1958 Convention on the High Seas entered into force on September 30, 1962, by a government the agents or instrumentalities of which are maintaining a registration of a vessel that is included on such list.

"(c) INFORMATION AND PUBLICATION.—The Secretary of the department in which the Coast Guard is operating, with the concurrence of the Secretary of State, shall—

"(1) maintain timely information on the registrations of all foreign vessels over 300 gross tons that are known to be—

"(A) owned or operated by or on behalf of the Government of North Korea or a North Korean person;

"(B) owned or operated by or on behalf of any country in which a sea port is located, the operator of which the President has identified in the most recent report submitted under section 205(a)(1)(A) of the North Korea Sanctions and Policy Enhancement Act of 2016; or

"(C) owned or operated by or on behalf of any country identified by the President as a country that has not complied with the applicable United Nations Security Council resolutions (as such term is defined in section 3 of such Act); and

"(2) not later than 180 days after the date of the enactment of this section, and periodically thereafter, publish in the Federal Register a list of the vessels described in paragraph (1).

"(d) NOTIFICATION OF GOVERNMENTS.—

"(1) IN GENERAL.—The Secretary of State shall notify each government, the agents or instrumentalities of which are maintaining a registration of a foreign vessel that is included on a list published under subsection (c)(2), not later than 30 days after such publication, that all vessels registered under such government's authority are subject to subsection (a).

"(2) ADDITIONAL NOTIFICATION.—In the case of a government that continues to maintain a registration for a vessel that is included on such list after receiving an initial notification under paragraph (1), the Secretary shall issue an additional notification to such government not later than 120 days after the publication of a list under subsection (c)(2).

"(e) NOTIFICATION OF VESSELS.—Upon receiving a notice of arrival under section 4(a)(5) from a vessel described in subsection (b), the Secretary of the department in which the Coast Guard is operating shall notify the master of such vessel that the vessel may not enter or operate in the navigable waters of the United States or transfer cargo in any port or place under the jurisdiction of the United States, unless—

"(1) the Secretary of State has made a determination under subsection (a)(2); or

"(2) the Secretary of the department in which the Coast Guard is operating allows provisional entry of the vessel, or transfer of cargo from the vessel, under subsection (f).

"(f) PROVISIONAL ENTRY OR CARGO TRANSFER.— Notwithstanding any other provision of this section, the Secretary of the department in which the Coast Guard is operating may allow provisional entry of, or transfer of cargo from, a vessel, if such entry or transfer is necessary for the safety of the vessel or persons aboard.

"(g) RIGHT OF INNOCENT PASSAGE AND RIGHT OF TRANSIT PASSAGE.—This section shall not be construed as authority to restrict the right of innocent passage or the right of transit passage as recognized under international law.

"(h) FOREIGN VESSEL DEFINED.—In this section, the term 'foreign vessel' has the meaning given that term in section 110 of title 46, United States Code.".

(b) CONFORMING AMENDMENTS.—

(1) SPECIAL POWERS.—Section 4(b)(2) of the Ports and Waterways Safety Act (33 U.S.C. 1223(b)(2)) is amended by inserting "or 16" after "section 9".

(2) DENIAL OF ENTRY.—Section 13(e) of the Ports and Waterways Safety Act (33 U.S.C. 1232(e)) is amended by striking "section 9" and inserting "section 9 or 16".

SEC. 316. REPORT ON COOPERATION BETWEEN NORTH KOREA AND IRAN.

(a) IN GENERAL.—Not later than 180 days after the date of the enactment of this Act, and annually thereafter for 5 years, the President shall submit to the appropriate congressional committees and leadership a report that includes—

(1) an assessment of the extent of cooperation (including through the transfer of goods, services, technology, or intellectual property) between North Korea and Iran relating to their respective nuclear, ballistic missile development, chemical or biological

weapons development, or conventional weapons programs;

(2) the names of any Iranian or North Korean persons that have knowingly engaged in or directed—

(A) the provision of material support to such programs; or

(B) the exchange of information between North Korea and Iran with respect to such programs;

(3) the names of any other foreign persons that have facilitated the activities described in paragraph (1); and

(4) a determination whether any of the activities described in paragraphs (1) and (2) violate United Nations Security Council Resolution 2231 (2015).

(b) FORM.—The report required under subsection (a) shall be submitted in unclassified form but may contain a classified annex.

(c) APPROPRIATE CONGRESSIONAL COMMITTEES AND LEADERSHIP DEFINED.—In this section, the term "appropriate congressional committees and leadership" means—

(1) the Committee on Foreign Relations, the Committee on Banking, Housing, and Urban Affairs, and the majority and minority leaders of the Senate; and

(2) the Committee on Foreign Affairs, the Committee on Financial Services, the Committee on Ways and Means, and the Speaker, the majority leader, and the

minority leader of the House of Representatives.

SEC. 317. REPORT ON IMPLEMENTATION OF UNITED NATIONS SECURITY COUNCIL RESOLUTIONS BY OTHER GOVERNMENTS.

(a) IN GENERAL.—Not later than 180 days after the date of the enactment of this Act, and annually thereafter for 5 years, the President shall submit to the appropriate congressional committees and leadership a report that evaluates the degree to which the governments of other countries have knowingly failed to—

(1) close the representative offices of persons designated under applicable United Nations Security Council resolutions;

(2) expel any North Korean nationals, including diplomats, working on behalf of such persons;

(3) prohibit the opening of new branches, subsidiaries, or representative offices of North Korean financial institutions within the jurisdictions of such governments; or

(4) expel any representatives of North Korean financial institutions.

(b) FORM.—The report required under subsection (a) shall be submitted in unclassified form but may contain a classified annex.

(c) APPROPRIATE CONGRESSIONAL COMMITTEES AND LEADERSHIP DEFINED.—In this section, the term "appropriate congressional committees and leadership" means—

(1) the Committee on Foreign Relations, the Committee on Banking, Housing, and Urban Affairs, and the majority and minority leaders of the Senate; and

(2) the Committee on Foreign Affairs, the Committee on Financial Services, the Committee on Ways and Means, and the Speaker, the majority leader, and the minority leader of the House of Representatives.

SEC. 318. BRIEFING ON MEASURES TO DENY SPECIALIZED FINANCIAL MESSAGING SERVICES TO DESIGNATED NORTH KOREAN FINANCIAL INSTITUTIONS.

(a) IN GENERAL.—Not later than 180 days after the date of the enactment of this Act, and every 180 days thereafter for 5 years, the President shall provide to the appropriate congressional committees a briefing that includes the following information:

(1) A list of each person or foreign government the President has identified that directly provides specialized financial messaging services to, or enables or facilitates direct or indirect access to such messaging services for—

(A) any North Korean financial institution (as such term is defined in section 3 of the North Korea Sanctions and Policy Enhancement Act of 2016 (22 U.S.C. 9202)) designated under an applicable United

Nations Security Council resolution; or

(B) any other North Korean person, on behalf of such a North Korean financial institution.

(2) A detailed assessment of the status of efforts by the Secretary of the Treasury to work with the relevant authorities in the home jurisdictions of such specialized financial messaging providers to end such provision or access.

(b) FORM.—The briefing required under subsection (a) may be classified.

subtitle B—Sanctions with respect to human rights abuses by the Government of North Korea

SEC. 321. SANCTIONS FOR FORCED LABOR AND SLAVERY OVERSEAS OF NORTH KOREANS.

(a) SANCTIONS FOR TRAFFICKING IN PERSONS.—

(1) IN GENERAL.—Section 302(b) of the North Korea Sanctions and Policy Enhancement Act of 2016 (22 U.S.C. 9241(b)) is amended—

(A) in paragraph (1), by striking "and" at the end;

(B) in paragraph (2), by striking the period at the end and inserting "; and"; and

(C) by adding at the end the following new paragraph:

"(3) a list of foreign persons that knowingly employ North Korean laborers, as described in section 104(b)(1)(M).".

(2) ADDITIONAL DETERMINATIONS; REPORTS.—With respect to any country identified in section 302(b)(2) of the North Korea Sanctions and Policy Enhancement Act of 2016 (22 U.S.C. 9241(b)(2)), as amended by paragraph (1), the report required under section 302(a) of such Act shall—

(A) include a determination whether each person identified in section 302(b)(3) of such Act (as amended by paragraph (1)) who is a national or a citizen of such identified country meets the criteria for sanctions under—

(i) section 111 of the Trafficking Victims Protection Act of 2000 (22 U.S.C. 7108) (relating to the prevention of trafficking in persons); or

(ii) section 104(a) or 104(b)(1) of the North Korea Sanctions and Policy Enhancement Act of 2016 (22 U.S.C. 9214(a)), as amended by section 101 of this Act;

(B) be included in the report required under section 110(b) of the Trafficking Victims Protection Act of 2000 (22 U.S.C. 7107(b)) (relating to the annual report on trafficking in persons); and

(C) be considered in any determination that the government of such country has made serious and sustained efforts to eliminate severe forms of trafficking in persons, as such term is defined for purposes of the Trafficking Victims Protection Act of

2000.

(B) SANCTIONS ON FOREIGN PERSONS THAT
EMPLOY NORTH KOREAN LABOR.—

(1) IN GENERAL.—Title III of the North Korea
Sanctions and Policy Enhancement Act of 2016 (22
U.S.C. 9241 et seq.) is amended by inserting after
section 302 the following new sections:

"SEC. 302A. REBUTTABLE PRESUMPTION APPLICABLE TO GOODS MADE WITH NORTH KOREAN LABOR.

"(a) IN GENERAL.—Except as provided in subsection
(b), any significant goods, wares, articles, and
merchandise mined, produced, or manufactured wholly
or in part by the labor of North Korean nationals or
citizens shall be deemed to be prohibited under section
307 of the Tariff Act of 1930 (19 U.S.C. 1307) and
shall not be entitled to entry at any of the ports of the
United States.

"(b) EXCEPTION.—The prohibition described in
subsection (a) shall not apply if the Commissioner of
U.S. Customs and Border Protection finds, by clear and
convincing evidence, that the goods, wares, articles, or
merchandise described in such paragraph were not
produced with convict labor, forced labor, or
indentured labor under penal sanctions.

"SEC. 302B. SANCTIONS ON FOREIGN PERSONS EMPLOYING NORTH KOREAN LABOR.

"(a) IN GENERAL.—Except as provided in subsection (c), the President shall designate any person identified under section 302(b)(3) for the imposition of sanctions under subsection (b).

"(b) IMPOSITION OF SANCTIONS.—

"(1) IN GENERAL.—The President shall impose the sanctions described in paragraph (2) with respect to any person designated under subsection (a).

"(2) SANCTIONS DESCRIBED.—The sanctions described in this paragraph are sanctions pursuant to the International Emergency Economic Powers Act (50 U.S.C. 1701 et seq.) to block and prohibit all transactions in property and interests in property of a person designated under subsection (a), if such property and interests in property are in the United States, come within the United States, or are or come within the possession or control of a United States person.

"(c) EXCEPTION.—

"(1) IN GENERAL.—A person may not be designated under subsection (a) if the President certifies to the appropriate congressional committees that the President has received reliable assurances from such person that—

"(A) the employment of North Korean laborers does not result in the direct or indirect transfer of convertible currency, luxury goods, or other stores of value to the Government of North Korea;

"(B) all wages and benefits are provided directly to the laborers, and are held, as applicable, in accounts within the jurisdiction in which they reside in locally denominated currency; and

"(C) the laborers are subject to working conditions consistent with international standards.

"(2) RECERTIFICATION.—Not later than 180 days after the date on which the President transmits to the appropriate congressional committees an initial certification under paragraph (1), and every 180 days thereafter, the President shall—

"(A) transmit a recertification stating that the conditions described in such paragraph continue to be met; or

"(B) if such recertification cannot be transmitted, impose the sanctions described in subsection (b) beginning on the date on which the President determines that such recertification cannot be transmitted.".

(2) CLERICAL AMENDMENT.—The table of contents in section 1(b) of the North Korea Sanctions and Policy Enhancement Act of 2016 is amended by inserting after the item relating to section 302 the following new items:

"sec. 302a. rebuttable presumption applicable to goods made with north korean labor.
"Sec. 302B. Sanctions on foreign persons employing North Korean labor.".

SEC. 322. MODIFICATIONS TO SANCTIONS SUSPENSION AND WAIVER AUTHORITIES.

(a) EXEMPTIONS.—Section 208(a) of the North Korea Sanctions and Policy Enhancement Act of 2016 (22 U.S.C. 9228(a)) is amended in the matter preceding paragraph (1)—

(1) by inserting "201A," after "104,"; and

(2) by inserting "302A, 302B," after "209,".

(b) Humanitarian waiver.—Section 208(b) of the North Korea Sanctions and Policy Enhancement Act of 2016 (22 U.S.C. 9228(b)(1)) is amended—

(1) by inserting "201A," after "104," in each place it appears; and

(2) by inserting "302A, 302B," after "209(b)," in each place it appears.

(c) WAIVER.—Section 208(c) of the North Korea Sanctions and Policy Enhancement Act of 2016 (22 U.S.C. 9228(c)) is amended in the matter preceding paragraph (1)—

(1) by inserting "201A," after "104,"; and

(2) by inserting "302A, 302B," after "209(b),".

SEC. 323. REWARD FOR INFORMANTS.

Section 36(b) of the State Department Basic Authorities Act of 1956 (22 U.S.C. 2708(b)), is amended—

(1) in paragraph (9), by striking "or" at the end;

(2) in paragraph (10), by striking the period at the end and inserting a semicolon; and

(3) by adding at the end the following new paragraphs:

"(11) the identification or location of any person who, while acting at the direction of or under the control of a foreign government, aids or abets a violation of section 1030 of title 18, United States Code; or

"(12) the disruption of financial mechanisms of any person who has engaged in the conduct described in sections 104(a) or 104(b)(1) of the North Korea Sanctions and Policy Enhancement Act of 2016 (22 U.S.C. 2914(a) or (b)(1)).".

SEC. 324. DETERMINATION ON DESIGNATION OF NORTH KOREA AS A STATE SPONSOR OF TERRORISM.

(a) DETERMINATION.—

(1) IN GENERAL.—Not later than 90 days after the date of the enactment of this Act, the Secretary of State shall submit to the appropriate congressional committees a determination whether North Korea meets the criteria for designation as a state sponsor of

terrorism.

(2) FORM.—The determination required by paragraph (1) shall be submitted in unclassified form but may include a classified annex, if appropriate.

(b) STATE SPONSOR OF TERRORISM DEFINED.—For purposes of this section, the term "state sponsor of terrorism" means a country the government of which the Secretary of State has determined, for purposes of section 6(j) of the Export Administration Act of 1979 (50 U.S.C. 4605(j)) (as in effect pursuant to the International Emergency Economic Powers Act), section 620A of the Foreign Assistance Act of 1961 (22 U.S.C. 2371), section 40 of the Arms Export Control Act (22 U.S.C. 2780), or any other provision of law, is a government that has repeatedly provided support for acts of international terrorism.

subtitle C—General authorities

SEC. 331. AUTHORITY TO CONSOLIDATE REPORTS.

Any reports required to be submitted to the appropriate congressional committees under this title or any amendment made by this title that are subject to deadlines for submission consisting of similar units of time may be consolidated into a single report that is submitted to appropriate congressional committees pursuant to the earlier of such deadlines. The consolidated reports must contain all information required under this title or any amendment made by this title, in addition to all other elements mandated by previous law.

SEC. 332. RULE OF CONSTRUCTION.

Nothing in this title shall be construed to limit—

(1) the authority or obligation of the President to apply the sanctions described in section 104 of the North Korea Sanctions and Policy Enhancement Act of 2016 (22 U.S.C. 9214), as amended by section 311 of this Act, with regard to persons who meet the criteria for designation under such section, or in any other provision of law; or

(2) the authorities of the President pursuant to the International Emergency Economic Powers Act (50 U.S.C. 1701 et seq.).

SEC. 333. REGULATORY AUTHORITY.

(a) IN GENERAL.—The President shall, not later than 180 days after the date of the enactment of this Act, promulgate regulations as necessary for the implementation of this title and the amendments made by this title.

(b) NOTIFICATION TO CONGRESS.—Not fewer than 10 days before the promulgation of a regulation under subsection (a), the President shall notify and provide to the appropriate congressional committees the proposed regulation, specifying the provisions of this title or the amendments made by this title that the regulation is implementing.

SEC. 334. LIMITATION ON FUNDS.

No additional funds are authorized to carry out the requirements of this title or of the amendments made by this title. Such requirements shall be carried out using amounts otherwise authorized.

Attest:

*Speaker of the House
of Representatives.*

Attest:

*Vice President of the
United States and
President of the
Senate.*

www.ingramcontent.com/pod-product-compliance
Lightning Source LLC
Chambersburg PA
CBHW071307220526
45468CB00001B/296